# Autism: The Founding Writings of Hans Asperger

Edition, Comments, and Translation:

Dr. Kevin Rebecchi, PhD

1

**Books in English by the same author**

*(already released or coming soon)*:

Autistic children - George Frankl

Autistic children - Grunya Efimovna Sukhareva

Autistic children - Leo Kanner

Autistic children - Lorna Wing

Autistic children - Hans Asperger


- Who are the truly abnormal? Between genetic diversity, neurological variability, and social Darwinism

- Education in nature and forest schools

- Learning to read and write without school

- Reggio Emilia, an innovative pedagogy for early childhood

- Montessori, what you need to know: An analysis of the essentials

# TABLE OF CONTENTS

# FOREWORD

## A brief biography

Professor Hans Asperger was born in Vienna, Austria, in 1906, where he attended school. He was part of a movement of young Catholics (Bung Neuland), engaging in outdoor hikes and mountain excursions. He studied at the University of Vienna, earning his doctorate in 1931. He began working at the University Children's Clinic in Vienna, later becoming the director of the therapeutic education station within the same clinic in 1935. In 1935, he married Hanna Kalmon, and they had five children. During this time, he embarked on his work with autistic children, a term that appeared in a private correspondence from 1934 preserved by his daughter (Feinstein, 2010), and later in a paper from 1938, a translated version of which is included in this book, as well as in his postdoctoral thesis from 1943, published in 1944 (see Rebecchi, 2023, for a recent translated and annotated version). He then served as a military physician in Croatia and returned to work at the University Children's Clinic in Vienna in 1945.

After spending five years between 1957 and 1962 as the director of the pediatric clinic at the University of Innsbruck, he became the director of the pediatric clinic at the University of Vienna from 1962 to 1977. He became a member of the National Academy of Sciences in 1967, received an honorary doctorate from the University Clinic of Munich in 1972, and retired from clinical practice in 1977. He continued to give lectures, write articles, and passed away in 1980.

In the article by Czech (2018) titled "Hans Asperger, National Socialism, and 'race hygiene' in Nazi-era Vienna," the author argues that Hans Asperger was not a staunch opponent of National Socialism, contrary to long-standing beliefs. Drawing on contemporary publications and archival documents, Czech suggests that Asperger accommodated the Nazi regime, affiliated with organizations linked to the German National Socialist Workers' Party (but not the Nazi Party itself), publicly supported policies promoting "racial purity," including forced sterilizations, and actively participated in the child euthanasia program. Czech contends that the image of Asperger as a courageous advocate for his patients against Nazi euthanasia measures and other racial purity policies does not withstand historical evidence.

In her book "Asperger's Children: The Origins of Autism in Nazi Vienna" (Sheffer, 2018), Sheffer analyzes the relationship between autism and the Nazi regime. According to her, Hans Asperger, apart from being involved in Hitler's Third Reich racial policies, might have also been implicated in crimes against children. She argues that Asperger and his collaborators sought to transform certain "autistic" children into productive citizens, while others were sent to Am Spiegelgrund, one of the Reich's deadliest child euthanasia centers. She suggests that Hans Asperger's work was rooted in the racial purity ideologies of National Socialism and draws connections to the present, where atypical behaviors are still seen as pathological and "social skills" are considered essential in psychiatric treatment of children.

However, in her article "Non-complicit: Revisiting Hans Asperger's Career in Nazi-era Vienna" (Falk, 2020), Falk refutes the allegations against Hans Asperger, asserting that it's highly improbable that Asperger was aware of the T4 program (a Nazi euthanasia program for physically and mentally disabled individuals) when he referred patients to Am Spiegelgrund. Falk suggests that from 1938 to 1943, Asperger vigorously campaigned for his specialization, therapeutic education, to take precedence in diagnosing and treating disabled children over other areas promoting Nazi racial hygiene policies. Falk also states that Asperger did not belittle his patients, was not sexist, and his research and discoveries positioned him as a pioneer in the field of autism.

Moreover, Tatzer et al. (2022) examined accusations against Hans Asperger regarding his involvement in the Nazi child euthanasia initiative. After analyzing primary documents and transcripts related to Asperger's recommendations to the Am Spiegelgrund children's home in Vienna, notorious for killing disabled children, their research indicated that Asperger recommended 13 children to Am Spiegelgrund, and although two girls died, the recommendations were made before the euthanasia program was widely known. They indicate that their investigation does not provide evidence that Asperger was aware of the euthanasia program when making his recommendations, except for one death likely due to euthanasia. Therefore, their study concludes that there's no indication that Asperger deliberately participated in the euthanasia program when recommending the two deceased patients to Am Spiegelgrund.

Furthermore, Heijder (2021) notes that Sheffer's claims in her book are controversial and their accuracy is debated. He points out, for example, that Sheffer highlights that the term "Intelligenzautomaten" can be translated as "intelligent automatons" and would suggest a dehumanizing view of autism, where autistic individuals would lack social value and the capacity to learn. Heijder argues that Sheffer has decontextualized Hans Asperger's statements and his analysis reveals that Asperger's use of the term "Intelligenzautomaten" does not exclusively refer to intellectually deficient children but encompasses all autistic children. He also notes that Hans Asperger mainly focused on the difficulties autistic children faced in acquiring social habits and learning from adults, rather than on their social value. Heijder suggests that Sheffer made an irrelevant association between Hans Asperger's discussions of children unable to learn from adults and following only their own ideas and methods, and the Nazi label of "uneducable." Furthermore, in Heijder's view, Sheffer made another irrelevant association between what Asperger referred to as the "least favorable cases" (intellectually deficient autistic individuals) and the most disabled children in general. He states that descriptions of different cases in Asperger's works illustrate these points. He therefore questions Sheffer's interpretations, indicating that she distorts Asperger's statements and takes phrases out of context to support her claims.

Lastly, Fangerau (2020) explored the debates between historical reconstruction and personal memory regarding National Socialism, emphasizing the importance of a culture of discussion that recognizes the differences between personal testimonies and historical reconstructions without pitting them against each other. According to Fangerau, determining who was a Nazi or involved in the Nazi regime is extremely complex, categorizing individuals as active or passive participants is challenging, and thus establishing responsibilities is difficult. Fangerau underscores the need to broaden the perspective beyond a few identifiable key authors and to consider all those who supported or contributed to the dictatorship in various ways in order to understand how individuals, described as educated, respected, and humane by their contemporaries before or after the Nazi era, could participate in regime policies and reinforce them. This would lead to a better understanding of unexplained and persistent biographical tensions. Fangerau points out that the tensions surrounding Hans Asperger concern evaluating sources regarding his involvement or non-involvement in the selection and euthanasia of children by the Nazis and evaluating his ideological stance toward Nazi positions. According to Fangerau, the distinction between evidence and indications leads to divergent interpretations resulting in opposing views on his guilt. She emphasizes that moral questions arise from a contemporary perspective and cautions against projecting current values onto historical figures, emphasizing the need to focus on understanding the historical context and factors that influenced Asperger's thoughts and actions within the framework of medical history during the Nazi era.

## What do those who knew him have to say?

Gillberg (2023) reports a conversation he had with Hans Asperger's daughter, where she allegedly mentioned that their family had been visited multiple times by the Gestapo because her father was not a member of the Nazi Party. She described her father as reserved, clumsy, and having a strong interest in language, elements associated with the autistic personality that he himself described (see Lyons & Fitzgerald, 2007 for a discussion on this matter).

Professor Heinz Rothbutcher (1981) noted that Professor Hans Asperger emphasized the need to constantly find the right balance, conditioned by internal and external developments, and he quoted him in this regard:

> *"He who knows himself, who positions himself critically and responsibly, will also do what is right; and he who keeps the measure, who does not exceed it, lives in peace with himself and with the community".*

Franz Wurst (1982), an Austrian pediatrician who studied under Hans Asperger, said of him that he didn't merely repeat dogmatic opinions or use ready-made formulas and solutions, but rather endeavored to seriously and creatively account for changing facts. Wurst reported that Asperger held deep respect for each individual, possessed an excellent memory, and had an innate interest in literature, enabling him to use a differentiated vocabulary with precision. Wurst noted that engaging in discussions with him was both an intellectual and emotional pleasure, and that Asperger considered the pedagogical approach as fundamental and complementary to the medical approach. Hence, Hans Asperger stated that he believed a "solely medical approach to treating children (...) can only be effective to a certain extent" and that

> *"Only pedagogical methods in the broadest sense of the term can really improve people, or more precisely, can identify the best development alternatives available to a child and enable him or her to develop in that direction"* (Asperger, 1950, p. 105, quoted by Asperger Felder, 2000)

Finally, his daughter notes that in his postdoctoral thesis, unlike other publications of that time, there were few references to the spirit of the era, racial hygiene and eugenics concepts, and she reports statements from her father in a 1974 interview:

*"The Nazi era arrived, and it was clear to me, based on my previous life, that I could align with many "national" things, in quotes, but not with inhumanity. In therapeutic education, we deal extensively with disturbed children, those with mental disabilities. There is no other way but to recognize their value and to love them. What is their value? What is the value? They are part of a population, indispensable for certain tasks, but also for a country's ethics, as they teach us how one human owes to another. It is entirely inhumane, as manifested in dreadful consequences, to define the concept of "life without value" and draw conclusions from it. And as I have never been inclined to draw those conclusions, that is to report individuals with mental disabilities to health authorities, as we were tasked to do, it posed a rather dangerous situation for me. I must pay special tribute to my professor Hamburger, who, although a committed National Socialist, saved me twice from the hands of the Gestapo with strong personal commitment. He knew what my convictions were. He protected me with all his might, and I am very grateful to him".* (Asperger, 1974, quoted by Asperger Felder, 2008)

Finally, Asperger wrote (and you can find this passage in Chapter X on the difficulties of the gifted) that:

*"We must strongly counter those who use the term 'inferior' too readily. The recent periods should have taught us the profoundly inhumane, even deadly consequences that this inevitably leads to: the term 'unworthy of life'*

*is not far away then! Yet, individuals who adopted such an attitude were completely blind to the fact that they themselves, considering themselves racially and characteristically of high value, were profoundly abnormal individuals, marked by their cold and unreal ideology as well as certain other 'psychopathic' traits, thus excluding themselves from the circle of humanity. One of the most powerful men of that time spoke of 'beasts of intelligence' - was he mocking himself? "*.

## Conclusion

Personally, I share Fangerau's view; I find it highly dangerous, absurd, and irrelevant to judge the past - especially when it involves mere interpretations - through the lens of present values. I find it even more questionable that this scrutiny targets an individual on a socially charged topic rather than the entire population of a particular era (why Hans Asperger, who wasn't even a member of the German National Socialist Workers' Party, whereas many other scientists, intellectuals, or artisans were, and yet nothing is said about them?). Why are all the other brands, companies, and personalities that collaborated with the Nazis and have clear sources not treated the same way (e.g., Hugo Boss, Volkswagen, or Maria Montessori)? Why is this approach not also applied to the customs and practices of ancient Greece?

I have been working on this topic for several years, and I have read numerous books and articles in various languages (even if I don't necessarily cite them all). To me, Asperger's descriptions are a must-read to understand and question the concept of autism, as well as that of neurodiversity. Some individuals may choose not to use the name "Asperger" if they feel uncomfortable with it. Nevertheless, from a scientific, social, and cultural perspective, it would be truly detrimental to erase all these descriptions and work as if they never existed. I thus encourage all those interested in the subject, whether directly, indirectly, or not at all, to exercise critical thinking, to read contradictory writings, and not to overlook these texts, as there's a risk of obtaining an incomplete and restricted insight into the topic.

The texts in this work do not all directly concern autism, but readers can find information that sheds light on Hans Asperger's stance and approach in a cross-cutting manner. However, this does not mean that everything is important, interesting, or relevant, nor that one should turn a blind eye in the other direction. In chapters II and III of this work, for example (but not exclusively), Hans Asperger discusses psychosis, neurosis, projective tests, the phenomenon of transference, repression, the Id and the Ego, integrative approach, the unconscious, depth psychology... sensitized readers will recognize this as psychoanalysis, with highly questionable epistemological foundations. This is why I chose to incorporate it, allowing a balance to be struck between reverence and detestation, reason and emotion.

The texts in this work cover various subjects. First, I decided to begin the book with generalities about diagnosis and the foundations of medical discourse (chapters I and II) so that readers can understand Hans Asperger's approach and his medically anchored vision deeply rooted in education. Subsequently, I included five chapters more oriented towards psychopathology, with the last one focusing on autism descriptions from 1938 (chapter VII). I continued with chapters on childhood anxiety (chapter IX), addictions (chapter X), children's lies, thefts, and runaways (chapter VIII), followed by highlighting the challenges faced by gifted individuals and their differences from autistic individuals (chapter XI). Lastly, chapter XII addresses the differential diagnosis of autism (e.g., with deafness or intellectual disabilities), chapter XIII highlights Hans Asperger's attachment to the educational approach, and the final two chapters delve into Kanner's autism and Asperger's autism, which, in my opinion, are the most significant in this work. Hans Asperger's final text on autism particularly sheds light on the evolution of his perspective between his 1943 postdoctoral thesis and his death in 1980, questioning the relevance of using the term "disability" to describe these peculiarities. As he noted in 1944 and 1938, contrary to Kanner's observation of autism's rarity, "If one learns to pay attention to the characteristic expressions of the autistic person, this psychopathic disorder, especially to a milder degree, is not rare at all, even in children," and "everything that deviates from the ordinary, thus 'abnormal,' must not necessarily be 'inferior' as a result."

I'd also like to point out (which can easily be corroborated based on descriptions by those close to him, similar to the analysis by Lyons & Fitzgerald, 2007) that I believe Hans Asperger was genuinely concerned with what he described. Otherwise, he wouldn't have managed to convey all these characteristics with such clarity and accuracy. Thus, I'll conclude with this sentence extracted from his 1944 postdoctoral thesis: "they have a particularly keen sense for the abnormality of other children; indeed, as abnormal as they may be themselves, they are positively hypersensitive to it."

## Nota Bene 1

It is important to bear in mind that these are primarily medical

14

and historical texts, and thus terms such as "suffering from," "affected by," "feeble," "stupid," "normal," "abnormal," "retarded," etc., are used. I have chosen not to alter these terms, and I encourage readers to step back from the phrasing and focus on the ideas.

## Nota Bene 2

Readers will notice that the author uses the third person singular to refer to himself on several occasions. This could be due to Germanic linguistic peculiarities and/or the posthumous addition of elements to his writings.

## References

Asperger, H. (1950). Die medizinischen Grundlagen der Heilpädagogik. Mtschr. f. Kinderhk. Band 99, Heft 3, S. 105-107

Asperger, H. (1974). Radiosendung: Geschichte und Geschichten, Transkript: Eva Skripsky, Matthias Huber; Archiv Maria Asperger Felder.

Asperger Felder, M. (2000). Foreword. In A. Klin, F. R. Volkmar, & S. S. Sparrow. Asperger Syndrome. The Guilford Press.

Asperger Felder, M. (2000). "Zum Sehen geboren, zum Schauen bestellt", Hans Asperger (1906-1980: Leben und Werk). In R. Castell. Hundert Jahre Kinder- und Jugendpsychiatrie. V&R unipress.

Czech H. (2018). Hans Asperger, National Socialism, and "race hygiene" in Nazi-era Vienna. *Molecular autism, 9*, 29. https://doi.org/10.1186/s13229-018-0208-6

Falk, D. (2020). Non-complicit: Revisiting Hans Asperger's Career in Nazi-era Vienna. *Journal of autism and developmental disorders, 50*(7), 2573–2584. https://doi.org/10.1007/s10803-019-03981-7

Feinstein, A. (2010). A History of Autism: Conversations with the Pioneers. Wiley–Blackwell.

Gillberg, C. (2023). Hans Asperger: True or not? *Acta Paediatrica.* https://doi.org/10.1111/apa.16697

Fangerau, H. (2020). Hans Asperger und der Nationalsozialismus: zwischen historischer Rekonstruktion und persönlicher Erinnerung. *Monatsschrift Kinderheilkunde, 168*(S3), 223–226. https://doi.org/10.1007/s00112-020-00952-6

Heijder, W. (2021). *A response to the book Asperger's Children by Edith Sheffer | University of Gothenburg.* https://www.gu.se/en/gnc/a-response-to-the-book-aspergers-children-by-edith-sheffer

Lyons, V., & Fitzgerald, M. (2007). Did Hans Asperger (1906–1980) have Asperger Syndrome? *Journal of Autism and Developmental Disorders, 37*(10), 2020–2021. https://doi.org/10.1007/s10803-007-0382-4

Rebecchi, K. (2023). Autistic children - Hans Asperger. Kindle Direct Publishing.

Rothbutcher, H. (1981). Foreword. In, H. Asperger & H. Rothbutcher. Das Rechte Mass. Selbstverlag der Internationalen Pädagogischen Werktagung.

Sheffer, E. (2018). Asperger's Children: The Origins of Autism in Nazi Vienna. W. W. Norton & Company.

Tatzer, E., Maleczek, W., & Waldhauser, F. (2022). An assessment of what Hans Asperger knew about child euthanasia in Vienna during the Nazi occupation. *Acta Paediatrica*. https://doi.org/10.1111/apa.16571

Wurst, F. (1982). Foreword. In, H. Asperger & H. Rothbutcher. Mit Konflikten Umgehen. Selbstverlag der Internationalen Pädagogischen Werktagung.

**Further information :**

La Gazette de l'autiste. (2023). Qui est Hans Asperger ? https://www.lagazettedelautiste.com/qui-est-hans-asperger

Silberman, S. (2015). NeuroTribes: The Legacy of Autism and the Future of Neurodiversity. Avery Publishing.

# I/ GENERAL INFORMATION ON DIAGNOSIS AND THERAPY (1982)

Who is this book intended for? First and foremost, it is aimed at pediatricians working in clinics and private practices, whose professional profile has significantly evolved, in our opinion, over the past decades. The private practice pediatrician is no longer primarily the assistant in infant feeding disorders and childhood infectious diseases; these problems can be considered resolved. Moreover, the catastrophic decline in births, which threatens the existence of the peoples of Central Europe, particularly endangers the pediatrician profession. Today, pediatricians are confronted with markedly different tasks: increasingly, children face difficulties in their upbringing and exhibit behavioral disorders ranging up to true neuroses. We are convinced that this is equally a consequence of the affluent and luxurious society as it is of its hostility towards children, a hostility that scarcely existed before. It is indeed a fact that children are often rejected and treated with incomprehension, even if this is denied with eloquent speeches.

The situation is similar for the general practitioner who treats children in their practice - this book concerns them as well. The changing clinical pictures observed by the pediatrician give rise to new important obligations for them, who should truly be the "defender of life" (Romano Guardini).

They must learn to recognize nervous and psychological disorders in children, ideally to prevent them - which would be the most beneficial - and to treat them with the methods that prove most effective in each case. It is often lamented that modern medical schools do not adequately teach such things to their students - they are fascinated by the successes of technological and overspecialized medicine; they have lost sight of the whole child, do not master the "school of observation," and therefore cannot teach it. They are not ready to examine the lived history of the child and understand their behavior.

However, we believe that this book could also be beneficial for other professions responsible for assessing children: psychologists (especially those working in clinical institutions), social workers who often play a decisive role in the fate of difficult children, but can only do so with precise knowledge of these children, as well as teachers, kindergarten educators, and caregivers.

It is fashionable today to consider education from an ideology and vehemently oppose them to each other. We believe that the practical result of these efforts is weak, and we believe, on the contrary, that we should follow nature as the teacher of education, of course, the nature to which both the physical and psychic dimensions of the child belong. Thus, this work will deal with natural realities, but how does one recognize them?

According to us, during observation, one should not orient oneself towards statistical norms, average values, but rather sharpen the gaze on what "stands out," on what is "different from expectation." Here is an example: the impression a child makes is different from what would correspond to their calendar age: proportions, big and small, like the shape of the face, dentition, contact, work mode, and other behaviors, all seem childish. If one follows this impression, both with precise measurements, targeted questions, and specific tests, if one recognizes, for example, delayed maturation (whatever its cause may be), this can lead to the heart of this child's problems. Thus, our approach starts from the remarkable, the unexpected, the specific, even the pathological. This approach has long been legitimate in medicine: pathology has always illuminated physiology, as disease is easier to understand than the much more complex fabric of the "normal," where the acting forces remain in dynamic equilibrium and are therefore invisible in their effectiveness; disease is, in fact, a pathological simplification of the normal. However, it is difficult for the psychologist and especially for the educator to follow this path, as both have been too educated in the concept of norms.

This work aims to demonstrate that this approach can also be fruitful for the educator by sharpening the focus on what stands out and by learning from child psychopathology.

The title of this book contains the term "heilpädagogik" (curative pedagogy). It first appeared in Austria in the mid-19th century in the work of Georgens, a teacher originally from Germany who worked in a home near Vienna. Based on his experience, he felt the need to also study medicine and work as both a physician and a teacher in the field of "work with the disabled," as we would say today. The need to integrate medical and educational aspects appears here, in our view, almost symbolically. This has remained true in Austria until today: unlike in other German-speaking countries, heilpädagogik here encompasses medical and biological thought and action as well as psychological issues and educational action. The necessity of not looking at each other with suspicion, in competition, in isolation, but of learning from one another, each learning from all the others, has persisted despite all the advances in knowledge and methods specific to each profession, and it must continue in this way for the well-being of the children entrusted to us.

Perhaps what is expressed in the first part of the compound word "heil-pädagogik" will then be realized: can pedagogical measures truly heal? The word may sound presumptuous to some, to the point that they want to completely abandon this term. But we believe that if the heilpädagoge, as we understand it, uses the means at their disposal, they can truly have a healing effect, just like a medical or psychotherapeutic treatment in a corresponding field. One must not forget that they work with children who, despite their disorders, can develop strengths that significantly improve their handicap, or even produce compensations and overcompensations. Time, with its patience combined with determination, is a powerful ally! How this can be achieved should be the content of this work.

The title "Psychotherapy and Early Childhood Heilpädagogik" demands a distinction between these two terms. The objectives certainly do not contradict each other: both aim to help and promote the development of children suffering from nervous and psychological disorders.

However, there are differences between the methods. Modern psychotherapy has developed a number of new treatments in addition to ancient classical treatments, which are described in this work. Heilpädagogik, when it incorporates medical and biological thinking (for example, knowledge of normal and pathological movements and resulting therapies for children with cerebral palsy, sensory impairment problems, or learning disorders), has also found a number of very effective specific methods. It is certain that children will benefit the most when the two approaches, that of psychiatry and pediatrics ("neuropediatrics") on one hand, and that of pedagogy on the other, collaborate effectively.

# II/ THE MEDICAL CONVERSATION (1982)

The conversation with the child holds significant diagnostic and therapeutic importance. It allows one to form an idea of the child's personality and to have a decisive influence on them, positioning oneself as a guide and support alongside them. It is important to clarify from the outset that a conversation fundamentally differs from a psychological test: in the latter, standardized demands must be presented to each child, using the same material, the same words, within a defined timeframe, in order for the results to be compared (it should be noted that there is a certain weakness in testing methods, especially intelligence tests, which fail to sufficiently individualize, providing only a quantitative measure despite attempts at differentiation based on various sub-scores—such as between the "verbal" and "performance" parts of the "Hamburg-Wechsler Test").

However, medical conversation, in order to fulfill its function, must be conducted very differently. It should not be standardized in any way (for example, by using a strictly followed questionnaire format). Its results are only generated through the communication between the unique person of the physician and that of the child.

## Contact development

It is appropriate to describe here how contact, especially verbal contact, develops systematically in children. The newborn, "without cortex," and the infant in the first months of life do not yet possess the capacity to understand language and produce it themselves. However, from the very beginning, the young child is capable, through their innate instinct, of perceiving the expressions of others and making themselves understood through unambiguous expressive manifestations—through mimicry, their gaze, which quickly becomes more differentiated and richer in communication possibilities, through vocalizations like cries expressed in various ways, and then, from the middle of the infantile period, through their experimental babbling that becomes progressively more expressive. Similarly, even the very young child is capable of "understanding" what is being offered to them in terms of humanity: the mother's caresses and warm embraces, her gentle whispers and songs, well before comprehending the meanings of words. The child's gaze and smile are the first signs of an intention to engage with others, especially the mother, with whom the child forms a "dyad," a unit (René Spitz) during the first few months. At the end of the first year, a developmental milestone occurs that elevates the child far above other mammals: language becomes intelligible to them, and they are capable of producing language themselves; the realm of the mind opens up, with language as its garment.

However, it must not be forgotten that the newly acquired ability to engage with the world verbally does not erase the "old" possibilities of relating to the environment, particularly the human environment, from a phylogenetic and ontogenetic perspective, but rather "integrates" them with the new (what was before remains "intact"). Understanding and producing these expressive manifestations remain essential for expressing consent or rejection, commands and obedience (something that intellectual psychology, which only follows the sense of words, neglected for a long time). We believe that these considerations presented constitute an important foundation for the very issue of medical conversation.

The experienced individual quickly realizes the child's capacity and willingness to engage: how they enter and take their place in space, how they look at adults with anxiety or confidence, how they respond to questions. During normal development, the child has developed highly differentiated verbal contact behavior, encompassing the foreign and the familiar, sympathy or antipathy (which clearly involve evaluating the interlocutor), superiority or inferiority, respect or stubborn resistance—in short, a rich range of relationships is expressed.

## Contact disorders: autism

These contact disorders are quite distinct – and have significant diagnostic relevance – from normal behavior in conversing with children, and they must be identified by the experienced physician and integrated into the child's personality profile. H. Asperger extensively described the peculiarities of conversational contact with autistic children, this self-referential (autos) withdrawal, the lack of understanding or rejection of contact with others, clearly manifested by avoiding eye contact and looking elsewhere, as well as through intonation idiosyncrasies, especially in word choice and sentence structure (in intellectually gifted autistics, there exists an early affinity with grammar and with language as a tool of abstraction). It is crucial to note that, in autistic children, language is not as much a means of contact, a "response" (what a magnificent expression in the German language!), but rather a "spontaneous language": the child doesn't consider whether they are being listened to or not, whether it's appropriate to speak in a certain way here and now – or not; they "resonate in space," proclaiming their own sometimes quite absurd ideas. The disturbance of verbal contact is even more severe in children described by L. Kanner as having "early infantile autism," a psychotic state in which language sometimes develops late and incompletely, or not at all. It's not used because contact is rejected or because the children don't understand it. (The significance of language in the structure of personality is also illustrated by the fact that these children's future is considerably dependent on their ability to "learn" a language, preferably through behavioral methods).

## Lack of distance

There are also completely opposite behavior disorders that manifest in conversations with children: it's inherent to genuine contact to always maintain the appropriate distance from the partner (it's interesting to trace the development of this distancing behavior – from the child's stranger anxiety at around five months, referred to by R. Spitz as the "eight-month anxiety," through increasingly differentiated distancing, which simply indicates that the child "draws contours around itself," becoming more aware of its own identity). However, there are children – often associated with an "organic brain psychosomatic syndrome," especially with epilepsy – who lack any understanding of the necessary distance from their partner. They become immediately "familiar," speak without concern, are undeterred by the partner's maintaining and requesting distance through their gaze. They stand out completely among peers and in relation to the teacher's authority, and their behavior can become unbearable: the lack of distance is a serious disruption in interpersonal relationships!

## Language and intelligence

We have already examined a child's conversational behavior from the perspective of contact and interpersonal communication. Now, let's talk about the intellectual characteristics that are expressed in language. An expert can form an idea of a child's intelligence without even conducting an in-depth test.

There are articulation disorders (stuttering, sometimes limited to certain sounds like S or R), there is the inability to form grammatically correct sentences corresponding to the developmental age (agrammatism) – this is more strongly correlated with intellectual deficit than the previous disorder. But more subtle criteria must also be applied to the child's language: what is the extent of their vocabulary, how are sentences structured in a differentiated manner? How do they express logical hierarchy? How do they understand questions and implied meanings? How sharp are their responses? What is their grasp of humor?

The criteria examined so far, which provide information about the child's contact and intelligence, already tell us a lot about their personal qualities. But we must go even further in our effort to clearly understand, during a conversation, the individual characteristics of the child and the current problems arising from their lived experience.

## Conducting the conversation

Here, any fixed pattern would fail. Young children cannot, and older ones often do not want to verbalize what deeply troubles them. Sometimes, they "play" (play therapy), or indications of such central problems can be obtained from a "projective" test (like the scene test). But even a well-conducted conversation can be more revealing than some tests (where there's always a risk of interpreting something not present in the child!).

How this happens isn't easy to describe. By observing the child's appearance, behavior, and language level, one already gets a certain idea of their content and intellectual interests. Then, questions are "asked" to deepen and specify this understanding, confirming one's own intuition or trying a different direction. It will often be advantageous to first address the child's interests and abilities: they can showcase what they can do, achieve successes, and feel the interviewer's interest. Once trust is established, the child's personal problems come into play – and that's when it becomes challenging!

It's difficult for a child to speak about what troubles them – they can't verbalize because it's unclear, they hide their fear and helplessness, and they're often under intense pressure from adults. A typical example: the tragic fate of children of divorced parents. After serious conflicts during their marriage, from which no child emerges unscathed, the parents finally live apart; the child is entrusted to the parent who can ensure their well-being (as far as the guardian judge can determine). But the problem is certainly not resolved! This parent who now "possesses" the child often uses them as a weapon against the still hated former partner, alienating the child's love for the father (the child is often with the mother) and poisoning them with the hatred that already caused the marriage to fail. How can a child defend against this, how can they even understand the game being played with them? They suffer and are afraid and can't handle it alone. At school, they talk about the father with pride in front of others, learn the Fourth Commandment, but the father is the enemy!

That was an example among many others. The doctor, whether requested as an expert by the guardianship court or consulted by the mother for the child's nervous (truly "psychosomatic") disorders, has significant opportunities regarding diagnosis and therapy. If he is a man, he is often perceived and accepted by the child, who has been so harshly disappointed until now, as a "father figure" if the interlocutor has given the child the feeling, through previous questions, that they could trust him and confide in an understanding and empathetic person (of course, a female doctor has similar chances if she knows how to use them). This is where the "transference phenomena" described so masterfully by Sigmund Freud come into play.

## The art of midwifery

Socrates brilliantly described his method of conducting conversations and interrogations as an "art of the midwife," and that corresponds to reality, as it "gives birth" to a living being, a spiritual being, just as a midwife gives birth to a newborn. After the dialogue, the situation is different for the questioner and the respondent: the questioner has advanced in their understanding of the child and their situation, and is now better equipped to help; the questioned child, who has been aided in expressing (!) themselves through empathetic questions, has freed themselves from many things they could not or did not want to express before. But they have also progressed on the path of their own self, self-awareness – and this, as will be further developed, is already a significant part of therapy!

The difficulties in conducting a fruitful conversation are not insignificant for both parties. The doctor naturally holds authority in their favor, and that helps immensely: they are assumed to understand everything – creating trust, especially if the child feels recognized through the preceding questions and thus is willing to open up further, even to their most intimate personal sphere. But authority can also be overwhelming to the extent that the child closes themselves off to the questioner. In this case, it will be helpful for the questioner not to adopt a superior attitude, but to reveal themselves through their tone, expression, and words as someone who stands beside the child, appreciates them, and advocates for them.


## Commitment to children

Often, the child believes that their parents have taken them to the doctor to have their head washed because of their "naughtiness" and other vices, and sometimes the child is correct, as their parents have instructed them as such. Therefore, it's not surprising that the child becomes stubborn, refuses to speak, or even throws a tantrum, driven by both rebellion and fear. Especially if the child is older and receptive to reasonable words, it must be firmly communicated to them that they are cared for, that assistance is wanted for their difficulties, and that support will also be given when they are believed to be right.

The examples mentioned above illustrate the difficulty a child can have in verbally expressing themselves before an inquiring doctor – on one hand, because they haven't yet reached the developmental stage enabling them to describe internal processes in response to revealing questions. The range of abilities is very wide at this stage; some children, especially gifted autistic children, already possess a surprisingly complete self-awareness from early childhood and are also ready to discuss and debate it. Others, however, even in adolescence when such problems generally surface, can't clarify their situation through language, even if attempts are made to assist.

Other obstacles exist. Fear that arises from within or from external situations hinders the child's verbal expression, or even prevents them from "thinking," from being able to perceive facts and report them. What has just been discussed relates to the psychoanalytic concept of "repression," though we wish to critically emphasize that what lies in the background, like remnants of "traumatic" experiences, isn't always fully "repressed" into the unconscious (which is often the case with adults as well). Rather, the child simply doesn't want to acknowledge it, doesn't want to confront it, even though they "know" very well. The doctor conducting the conversation must then encourage the child to recognize this and to express themselves more clearly, carefully seeking their words. This is a true "birthing process," in the sense of the Socratic comparison! It's fascinating to observe how awareness emerges in a child (Viennese psychologist Karl Bühler aptly spoke of an "Aha experience"), how sometimes, in an untaught, unconditioned, but "natural" and creative language, a successful formulation arises that is then liberating. However, this occurs through a process of communication between the questioner and the respondent, benefiting both significantly: for the conversing doctor, an image of a personality with abilities and difficulties, with conflicts where the child needs help, takes shape – for the child, a good conversation is an important part of therapy. This is what needs to be discussed further.

## The therapeutic effect of conversation

Plato, the student of Socrates, founded his philosophy on demonstrating how knowledge unfolds through the interplay of questions and answers between the student and the master, subsequently aiding individuals to live well and guiding the social community towards a higher order. The same phenomenon occurs in the encounter between the child and the experienced and compassionate doctor. Suddenly, the child comprehends the connections between events that previously tormented them because they were only confused and misunderstood, threatening and frightening – and they recognize themselves, their role in this often disastrous game. This aligns perfectly with Freud's words that psychotherapy aims to "transform the Id into the Ego," into a grateful and responsible self.

The behavior described for the conversation leader distinguishes itself from an approach that imposes prescriptions or preaches morality to the child. As they say, such words "go in one ear and out the other," not truly affecting the child's motivations. Hence, we assert that the only behavior befitting a therapist is rooted in respect for the child; one shouldn't attempt to "manipulate" them (which is why we also oppose the often intrusive "behavioral therapy" of our times, which seems too mechanistic to us with its positive and negative reinforcements, providing too little room for the child's freedom; we deem this approach acceptable only for severely affected children, for instance, those with organic brain conditions). Respect towards the child means: listening attentively to what the child says, giving them time to think, offering them the chance to clarify matters by posing questions if they are uncertain, refraining from imposing interpretations (which impatient analysts often do!). It also means being skeptical of overly common promises of improvement or empathically displayed "realizations." A genuine realization, emerging in a child through the course of conversation, is manifested through sudden silence, hesitation, or introspection (as signs of internal reflection), rather than through numerous commonplace words.

In our view, it's also respectful towards the child to hold back, as one never knows how the conversation's outcomes, what one says to the child, truly affect them. Many things that one has taken very seriously oneself often pass without an effect on the child. But sometimes, decades later, it's observed that an adult who has long since grown remembers: at the time, when they were a child, the doctor said a word to them that they haven't forgotten since, and it influenced their decisions – one themselves hadn't remembered for a long time!

What transpires in the conversational contact with the child seems to us to already encompass all that matters in psychotherapy and therapeutic education (incidentally, these two concepts do not differ in terms of objectives): engaging with a child, standing by their side, elucidating and directing, with respect for the child's personhood, and offering decisive assistance in what resonates within them from conversations, often fostering their development.

**<u>Conversation Contents</u>**

At the beginning of this chapter, we dismissed all schematization of conversation, as it would significantly disrupt the immediacy of communication. Nonetheless, it's appropriate to mention that certain issues probably arise in every conversation: school with its successes and failures, concerns and fears, task-related situations (the conversation must be conducted in a way that the child doesn't perceive themselves as a complete failure, so that the posed demands are elastic, adapted to their capacities without them noticing); interests outside of school (potential specific interests); intentionally later (so that the child already has trust), family issues are addressed, the relationship with both parents and potential educators, as well as with siblings (approaching all this patiently, noting both silence and speech); professional aspirations and ideas about future life conduct; in older individuals, attitudes towards love and sexuality, as well as experiences in this realm (here, moralizing is useless, even harmful, with understanding being essential!). All this is precisely tailored to the child's or adolescent's reactions, always being ready to find new approaches for each individual case.

One problem remains for which we cannot provide a solution: medical conversation, as we have attempted to describe it, demands a significant amount of time. And the practicing doctor, burdened with many other tasks, will struggle to find this time, often feeling on the brink of failure. Such is the fate of those who strive to display humanity, which is difficult to avoid. However, within certain limits, it is possible to streamline time, for example, by arranging dedicated consultations for conversations with a child, followed by discussions with the parents when one senses significant and perilous problems lurking beneath the surface. Nevertheless, the reproach of not having done enough always remains embedded in the medical conscience.

# III/ SUGGESTIVE THERAPY (1982)

## <u>Biological Foundations</u>

Suggestive therapy is a treatment method that generates various divergent opinions. Its foundation is supposed to arise from biological regularity, a principle that runs through this entire work. The autonomic nervous system, which governs the functioning of all our organs (its prominent researcher, L.R. Müller, speaks of the "nerves of life and vital impulses"), has long been known also as the "sympathetic nervous system." Indeed, this name predates the previously mentioned one, aiming to indicate opposition to the "animal nervous system." Sympathetic signifies that it suffers with, feels along with what transpires on the psychological plane in the human being; the psychological is physically expressed through vegetative functions, and psychic events influence all that is bodily.

While we are convinced that constitutional and hereditary factors play a role in vegetative dysfunctions leading to various organic disorders, there's no doubt, on the other hand, that errors in the family environment and later in the school environment play a causal role in the emergence of organic disorders, "organic neuroses," which will be described in detail in this work. Traumatizing experiences for the child are also spoken of; it is necessary to identify and eliminate them if one wishes to assist the child in improving their situation. And it is certain that if a disruptive environmental situation can lead to vegetative dysfunctions, it's also possible to achieve improvement, a return to normal function, by creating a better atmosphere, instilling trust, and eliminating fear, which will have a "sympathetic" effect on the child.

Suggestive therapy is one of the means to achieve this. It has an honorable lineage. Ancient medicine, practiced by physician-priests, sorcerers, in various forms, only worked with such means, and certainly not without success, as history shows. At that time, there were still few medications that could genuinely intervene in the body's chemistry. This has changed significantly in modern medicine, where we are capable of achieving decisive therapeutic effects by mastering biochemical processes. However, what occurs in the living organism is not entirely identical to processes in test tubes, largely due to influences of the autonomic nervous system. After a period of absolute belief in technology and chemistry, a salutary disillusionment has settled today. We've realized that what was effective in ancient medicine, namely faith in the healing power of the human being, always has decisive importance, even before "organic" effects. Critical studies, such as "double-blind trials," have clearly demonstrated the power of these factors (the critical evaluation of drugs now imperatively requires comparison with the effects of a "placebo" – this Anglo-Saxon term denoting a substance that does not chemically react with the organism, unlike the "real" medication, is also accepted in our language).

## Thymotropic Therapy

My professor Franz Hamburger termed a treatment that follows these principles "thymotropic therapy" – an apt term, I believe. It addresses the child's emotional realm (thymos); the child has confidence in the healing power of the doctor, and it is precisely this that prompts a modification in the organism, improving or causing the painful symptoms to disappear, particularly at the level of certain organs. Just like with everything involving the child, the mother is also "in play." One should never tell the mother that the medication or treatment used does not intervene "truly" in the pathological process. On the contrary, she should, like the child, be convinced of the efficacy of the prescribed measures and reflect this conviction to the child. If things were different, if she had doubts, the therapy would certainly be ineffective for the child. In this sense as well, the mother and child form a unit, a deeply rooted unity, far deeper than mere intellectual understanding, more profound, namely in the "thymic" domain. The doctor must be aware of this and take it into account; they must also convince the mother and under no circumstances tell her that it's a "placebo treatment."

## Technique

Regarding the procedure, the doctor prescribes a medication, preferably specially prepared for the occasion and not pre-packaged (as in this case, the mother would certainly scrutinize the instructions and compare them with the medical advice), and provides precise instructions on how to use the medication several times a day. If the mother and child diligently follow these instructions, it brings them stability and confidence. Increasing the "dose" of the medication if improvement isn't rapid and intense enough is an important "reinforcer" (to use the jargon of modern behavioral therapy, which has some similarities with suggestive treatment); if it works, both the mother and child see it as evidence that the medication dose was correct.

The dose will be reduced as symptoms improve, and the treatment won't be terminated prematurely; rather, efforts will be made to consolidate progress by extending the treatment duration. The diverse experience of individuals working with such therapy proves its effectiveness. Particularly, "organic neuroses" respond well to this type of treatment: dysfunctions of the bladder and rectum (diurnal and nocturnal enuresis, encopresis), "nervous" cough and respiratory disorders, as well as tics (although the treatment is often challenging—indeed, even with neurological medications!), sleep disorders, including difficulties falling asleep (which is understandable considering how much this process depends on mood!); a wide range of symptoms affects the gastrointestinal tract, such as appetite disorders, vomiting, and pain; other conditions affect circulation, which Hamburger termed "attention neuroses." Excessive concern about heart rate is observed, and at that very moment, it is already disturbed, leading to painfully felt arrhythmias.

## Mode of Action

If the doctor manages to improve or eliminate such symptom patterns with the described method, they will have provided significant help—not only to the child who was greatly troubled by it, but also to the family who was distressed and facing significant difficulties.

Think about the emotionally distressing work imposed on the mother who constantly has to rearrange the child's clothes and bed linen due to bedwetting or accidents!

However, such treatment doesn't just work in a "symptomatic" manner; it goes much further. Very often, organic symptoms are fueled, caused, and perpetuated by anxiety (especially enuresis and encopresis, but also many other patterns of "psychosomatic" diseases). The trust established with the doctor in a successful treatment, which is actually the effective element, also acts dynamically against the anxiety of the child and mother. During therapy, there is generally increased attention from the mother towards her child, and this too is directly beneficial. If suggestive treatment is well-conducted—which of course requires the doctor to see the child and mother repeatedly and provide continuous "support"—it transforms into a kind of "family therapy" that can genuinely improve significantly distressing family issues.

## Limits and Dangers of Suggestive Therapy

If one wants to serve the truth, which means presenting problems as complex and contradictory as they really are, it must be acknowledged that suggestive therapy has its limits, which must be respected. On one hand, the person being treated in this manner knows too little about the child, their personal structure, but especially about the traumatic situation in which they are growing up. It wouldn't be beneficial for success if the doctor asks too many questions. Presenting oneself as capable of doing the work, understanding the disorders, without having to ask many questions; asking in-depth and patient questions contradicts the attitude of someone using such methods, and it might even arouse suspicion towards such a doctor.

However, someone who acts as an authority, without asking questions and demanding trust from others, risks missing out on a lot! They might overlook what's detrimental in the background. An example: a child wets themselves at school or vomits regularly before school because they are completely overwhelmed by an inept teacher or due to a general or specific mental delay. It's possible that the complaints disappear for a while due to suggestive treatment. But the problem isn't solved! It's likely that the same symptoms or other symptoms will reappear, even more oppressive than before: one can also temporarily alleviate headaches caused by a brain tumor with a suggestive-effect methodology—but they will surely come back, with other manifestations; however, valuable time for real etiological treatment will have been lost!

This also illustrates how dangerous it is to conceal things and neglect what's necessary. Schools of depth psychology have accused suggestive therapy of being "superficial," of merely masking symptoms and their causes, of not contributing to genuine understanding—and this accusation isn't entirely unfounded. In difficult conflict situations, a "revealing" process is needed that seeks to understand causal links. And what may seem at first to be an advantage for the overburdened doctor with appointments: the relative ease of suggestive therapy (precisely what it also recommends to the child and mother), is a major drawback in a complicated case. It takes time, it requires asking questions in many directions to truly understand a child and their situation. And a second important objection to this treatment: what's really happening? Treatment is carried out with medications and procedures that have no "inherent effect," but depend on "thymic change" (which can be sufficiently effective). But isn't such a method a deception? Doesn't it border on quackery? The critical doctor must have the same doubts, even when they believe they are treating "rationally," by acting on the body's chemistry; they never know how much of the results are actually due to the placebo effect. Thus, what the great doubter and questioner Faust resignedly says during his Easter walk remains valid: "Oh, happy is he who still can hope," (he himself no longer hopes!), "emerging from this sea of errors! What you don't know, you need, and what you know, you can't use."

However, it's certain that dealing with suggestive methods is a borderline situation with considerable dangers, where one risks drifting towards hasty affairs, towards deceiving others and oneself, towards ignorance of real problems (which can be deadly in the case of organic illness, but no less fatal in the case of psychogenic disorders).

## Overestimation of the Problem

Nevertheless, the doctor must learn and possess the ability to navigate in borderline situations. They must make decisions and intervene in the destinies of others, precisely when the danger is high. And they must confront constant doubt and even use this doubt to refine their judgment. Certainly, it is nobler to guide a child towards self-discovery through the "midwifery" art of conversation, appealing to their freedom. But this isn't always possible; it also depends on the child's age and their capacity for critical thinking. In such cases, resorting to suggestive therapy is justified. However, this entails making decisions on behalf of the child and the mother, taking charge of the child (which means "manipulating").

It's not easy for the doctor to keep their hands clean in this process. They must resist the temptation of easy gain, precisely respect the boundaries within which they can "manage" the other, including a child; and finally, as challenging as it may be during such treatment, they must seek to understand the child in their structure and conditions (and in reality, the child's reaction at different stages of therapy provides important insights into their nature). A good approach is to strive, after successful suggestive therapy, when a tormenting symptom has disappeared and trust has been established, to humanely care for the child and their family "beyond the symptom."

Another difficulty is to describe. Undoubtedly, the doctor who achieves the best results is the one who not only presents themselves convincingly externally but is also convinced of the effectiveness of their treatment themselves.

Hamburger coined the term "thymic automatism": healing processes unfold almost automatically, without his intervention, if only the doctor is properly attuned in the "deep zone" (in the thymos) of their personality. However, this poses real challenges for the critical doctor: they know they are ultimately conducting a fictitious treatment, but they must present it convincingly to others.

For this, the doctor must be in control of themselves to be able to instill trust in the child and the mother. Certainly, it's a high goal for them to represent the truth. However, the question of what is acceptable to the other, what must be concealed from them here and in many other problems, is a vast realm of decisions that the doctor must make from the core of their person, from their professional ethics that result from their freedom and commitment. The methodology of suggestive therapy is part of this circle of decisions as an important psychotherapeutic method with which the doctor can act in accordance with the claim to provide assistance.

# IV/ BRAIN-BASED PSYCHIC SYNDROME (1982)

Manfred Bleuler, an eminent figure and grandson of a distinguished grandfather (Eugen Bleuler, a Zurich psychiatrist, creator of ingenious terms like "schizophrenia" and "autism"), described in the 1950s the "cerebral origin psychic syndrome." The emphasis is on the first part of the word "psycho" in syndrome: it pertains not so much to neurological consequences like motor disorders (various forms of "cerebral palsy"), but rather to immediate psychological consequences following a cerebral illness, as well as enduring sequelae.

## Etiology

It's necessary to mention certain things regarding etiology in order to make a diagnosis. The possibilities for damage are numerous, spanning from early pregnancy throughout one's entire life. For prenatal damage, during the embryonic and fetal periods, there are various anamnestic clues: bleeding indicating imminent miscarriage, maternal hyperemesis, but most importantly, infections. Even a seemingly harmless "flu," almost forgotten by the mother, can seriously harm the fetus or embryo due to the viremia transmitted. "Rubella embryopathy," caused by maternal rubella infection during the first trimester of pregnancy, revealed a new realm of medical knowledge with severe malformations of the central nervous system and the organs derived from it, such as the eyes and ears. An important indicator is "prenatal dystrophy" (underdevelopment despite a normal or even extended gestational period: "small-for-date baby"). Then, there are numerous possibilities for traumatic birth injuries (not only severe brain damage and massive hemorrhages, but especially various forms of perinatal asphyxia); information about the infant's behavior in the early days of life is important: deviations from norm in terms of motor activity, restlessness or apathy, sleep disturbances, feeding difficulties, various forms of seizures. Furthermore, congenital malformations of the central nervous system and its vascular system, whether isolated as pore malformations, cortical deformations, or within more generalized disorders with ocular, auditory, facial, cardiac, and renal malformations, play a numerically significant role under the label of "malformative retardation syndromes." After birth, various types of traumatic and inflammatory disorders also occur (meningitis and encephalitis, with the disturbing rise of viral-origin encephalitis being a phenomenon observed in all developed countries).

The ensuing states are in no way determined by the type of cause: states determined by inflammation or damage can provoke exactly the same patterns. It's also challenging to recognize specific patterns based on the location of lesions in the brain, especially as they are generally multiple lesions. However, the extent of lesions, the degree of destruction of ganglion cells and neurons, naturally determine the nature and degree of ensuing psychological states. As Manfred Bleuler aptly highlights in his fundamental work: "One can speak of a symptomatological framework common to all local psychic syndromes of the brain."

# Physical Symptomatology

<u>Vegetative, Trophic, and Endocrine Signs</u>

Before discussing the ensuing psychological states, some indications about the symptomatology need to be provided. Manifestations of the autonomic nervous system are frequent as consequences of cerebral lesions, with the most common being varying degrees of hypersalivation (saliva dripping from the mouth, leading to "wet speech," often associated with partial or total articulatory disturbances); the impression these children give is often also determined by gaze peculiarities: due to excessive lacrimal gland secretion, the eyes acquire an intensified gleam; this, coupled with a certain limitation of ocular mobility, gives rise to the impression of a "glassy-eyed" character - we call this symptom, recognizable to experienced individuals, the "encephalitic gaze." However, the opposite can also occur: an especially dull and lackluster gaze in individuals with cerebral impairments; and both extremes can alternate in a child.

Trophic disruptions of the body, visibly also governed by cerebral impulses, are equally intriguing. Individuals with cerebral impairments often exhibit a particular flexibility in finger joint articulations, or conversely, thickening of the distal phalanges of the fingers, or finally, the opposite: narrowing of the phalangeal extremities. Dental anomalies are common, but only in cases of acquired cerebral impairments very early in life: the teeth are thick, have a dense and opaque enamel; they are often highly dystopic, with grotesque deformations of dental alignment; then, there's early dental decay, so only tooth remnants are visible (if this concerns deciduous teeth, these teeth must have been affected during their formation, long before birth, indicating very early cerebral damage). Gingival hypertrophy is also frequent (this is observed not only during long-term antiepileptic medication but, in our opinion, also as a trophic disorder ultimately cerebral in nature).

Knowing that the highest regulation of endocrine circuits is located in subcortical regions, mainly in the diencephalon, and knowing also that encephalitis frequently occurs in these regions, one also understands that endocrine disorders are often caused by cerebral lesions. Following inflammations as well as cerebral traumas, symptoms are observed on the side of the thyroid (primarily hypothyroidism) as well as the pituitary gland (diabetes insipidus, growth hormone deficiency leading to growth cessation; possibly certain forms of diabetes mellitus). However, one should not automatically assume that these disorders, being caused by cerebral lesions, are not amenable to hormone therapy!

## Other Methods

We reiterate that in this section, we focus on the psychological aspect of cerebral disorders and abnormal behaviors. However, a brief mention of physical symptoms has been made to provide diagnostic indications and confirm the organic cerebral cause of abnormal behaviors. In such cases, it is, of course, necessary to explore all other avenues of knowledge: electroencephalography (EEG) (though it is worth noting that this examination method generally does not provide much information, except in cases of comorbidity with epileptic conditions); even the most advanced imaging method, computed tomography (CT), usually does not yield significant indications, particularly regarding localization. Anatomical modifications are generally limited and thus invisible. It is heartening to observe that the previously used methodology, pneumoencephalography, is now much less common as it caused considerable discomfort to children. Conversely, it seems that observing physical characteristics along with the autonomic system and motor movements yields the most information. Therefore, we must sharpen our observation skills.

## Disintegration and psychic particularities of children with organic brain disorders

If we search for the "common symptomatic framework," as Mr. Bleuler termed it, we believe we can find it in the fact that a psycho-organic syndrome leads to a disintegration of cerebral functions. Thus, it is not a failure of individual cerebral functions (for example, intellectual capacities can be normal, even superior, as a whole or in specific sub-functions). However, what is disrupted is the wonderful interaction that constitutes the unity of the human individual, capable of critically recognizing reality and responding responsibly to the situation. Nevertheless, in certain cases, it can be quite difficult to recognize this disorder of the psychic whole (precisely because we have known since Aristotle that the whole is more than the sum of its parts, that this whole is indivisible, "individual," and ultimately incomparable to others, which means that the human individual remains unknown to others and to their own self-examination - the "unknown person"). Since general disorders due to organic cerebral syndrome are so difficult to describe, for didactic reasons, we will first address specific disorders in individual domains, specific functions. These are also easier to recognize and describe. Much has recently been discussed about "partial performance disorders," especially disorders of shape perception, which can be effectively highlighted through various "shape tests." As this disorder also occurs in "minimal cerebral lesions," we will describe it in more detail in the next chapter.

## Activity Disorders

There are numerous disorders in the realm of activity. This can generally be diminished in the sense of torpor, with or without neurological symptoms: lethargy of impulses is observed with a slowing down and limitation of actions, to varying degrees ranging from pronounced post-encephalitic parkinsonism to slight limitations of activity, perceptible to an attentive observer through facial fluidity, temporal delays, quantitative and qualitative impoverishment of actions. More frequently after an organic cerebral lesion, an opposite activity disorder is found: excessive excitability, with a rapid succession of impulses. Behavioral motivations do not provide the appropriate response to situational demands: they exhaust rapidly, terminate abruptly, without any significant connection between them. We say that these children are composed of "fragments," that there is no guiding thread that ties individual moments together. Children are hypersensitive to incoming stimuli, as the "integrative" function that should select these stimuli based on the current situation is lacking. Eruptive activity manifests at various levels, which naturally depends on other personality qualities. Children with eruptive mental deficiency are tormented and pedagogically difficult to control. Their time is occupied by stereotypes that can hardly be qualified as "activities," endless oscillatory movements (do they play with a slight sensation of vertigo?), sometimes even self-inflicted blows to their bodies, head-banging against the wall (do they enjoy the sensation of pain?). However, more organized activities also exist, often still absurd, consisting of acts of malice (with some perception, they recognize what is particularly disturbing, particularly dangerous in a situation; electrical switches and water pipes are particularly appreciated). What they do is so serious that the mother precisely sees evidence of the child's intelligence in it - because he "knows" how serious his misdeeds are! This leads to increasingly organized activities that appear intelligent and effective, but when examining the circumstances and motivations closely, these actions show that they are not the right "response" to the "challenge," thus endangering the child themselves and their social environment, simply because proper integration of the individual is disrupted.

## "Kurzschlüssigkeit" (Short Circuit, Moment of Madness)

The activity of individuals with organic cerebral disorders ultimately has something "kurzschlüssig" - an appropriate expression, according to us. Normally, each action impulse is confronted with past experiences, while also taking into account considerations about what an action could become in the future, what its consequences might be (humans, the only creature that "has" time, integrates the past and the future in the instant of decision!). In decision-making, higher evaluations are also taken into account, movements of consciousness (or the "superego" according to the terminology of depth psychology), it is evaluated whether an action to be executed is allowed or forbidden according to divine or human laws. After such a long "process of instances," either the decision is made that the action is suitable, the right "response" to the situation's "challenge" (challenge and response, as A. Toynbee described human action in history in his magnificent work "A Study of History"), or the action is inhibited, suppressed. However, in individuals organically affected by the brain, even if their intelligence is perfectly intact, they often act in a "kurzschlüssig" manner: these higher integrations that render an action appropriate and responsible fail; the impulse immediately transforms into action. Just as in an electrical short circuit, bare wires touch each other "directly," the current takes this path in a destructive manner, kurzschlüssig activity has the same disruptive and destructive effect - as dangerous aggression in rapidly inflamed affect, as a criminal act where consequences are not considered at the "decisive moment" (of course, afterward, understanding and remorse are entirely possible if intelligence is not disrupted). Such processes can raise difficult issues in forensic psychiatry: what does "criminal responsibility" mean for certain individuals and acts? A precise analysis of the personality and the act is absolutely necessary.


## Affection

After describing the abnormal and "kurzschlüssig" activity of children with cerebral disorders, it is now appropriate to discuss "disintegration" in the affective and emotional domain. Once again, it should be noted that normally, emotional relationships between the child and others are "confronted with time": time is needed for the initial distance and shyness to transform into trust, provided that the other person has earned that trust, implying complex cognitive and decision-making processes in both partners.

It's heartening to observe how the child's gaze and facial expressions change as they grow closer to the other person.

But in a deeper sense, affective relationships are "engaged over time": they must be nurtured, honored with fidelity, and one knows oneself bound to them. Thus, the child refrains from doing wrong, refrains from taking challenging commitments so as not to sadden beloved parents, not to disappoint the admired teacher.

All of this is different in many disturbed cerebral cases. At first glance, the children do not seem to have emotional disorders: they adapt well emotionally to a situation, behave entirely synchronously, react immediately to joy and pain, appear to have easy rapport with others. However, these easily excitable emotions lack both duration and depth, they are too readily swept away by new experiences.

This can have very different consequences in individual cases: sometimes, it manifests as a lack of personal boundaries, excessive closeness to others, even intrusion—this breach of personal limits can be highly dangerous for a child; such types often become victims of sexual aggression, one could even say they magnetically attract such experiences. And other children with cerebral disorders, yet with certain constitutional and hereditary predispositions, retreat into themselves, react in an "autistic" manner (see this chapter!).

The influence of constitutional conditions is evident in many cases of organic brain personality disorders. It can be said that cerebral disorder exaggerates, amplifies pre-existing characteristics: children who behave autistically lack the distinctive aspect of the "autistic psychopaths" we have described, and on the other hand, children from primitive families become even more "primitivized."

This becomes perfectly understandable when considering what occurs in the diseased brain: cells and cellular connections are destroyed, the interconnection of functions is faulty—and when R. Lempp speaks of "connection disorders," he means the same thing. Once again, it's precisely these tragic cases that make us realize the marvel of normal personality integration, enabling humans to act freely and responsibly.


## <u>Relationship disorders</u>

Difficult problems arise in these children because the educational environment often behaves inappropriately, which only exacerbates the abnormal behavior of the children. There are legitimate links between the child's disorder and the inappropriate behavior of the mother, the educator. Interpersonal relationships are not only influences in one direction, that is, from the mother to the child. From a very young age - and this is particularly evident during this early period - the child also stimulates appropriate maternal behavior through their expressions, motor skills, facial expressions, gaze, triggering what is inherent in inherited maternal instinct.

In "comparative behavior research," we speak of "key stimuli" emanating from the child that precisely correspond to the "lock" in the mother.

The child with cerebral disorders is unable to emit the correct key stimuli, as is evident from the description of anomalies, particularly in the motor domain, but also in the child's activity and emotionality. Therefore, it's not surprising that the mother does not respond correctly to the child's behavior. She can't even rely on her maternal instinct!

The child with cerebral disorders, awkward and abnormal in their activity, in their maladaptation to practical aspects of life, does not seek independence in a healthy "functional drive" (Ch. Bühler) as a healthy child would (one who soon no longer seeks help for daily tasks, one who can't even be "spoiled"!). However, these children find themselves—or rather push the mother—into a situation of "overprotection"; the mother, overwhelmed by compassion for her poor child, tries to remove every pebble from their path, thus preventing the child from developing the strengths and capabilities they would indeed be capable of accessing.

Even in her emotional attitude towards the child, the mother is often uncertain, precisely because the child does not "play" correctly. Feelings of guilt ("how could I have caused the child's condition?"), rejection, even hatred towards the child, which does not contribute at all to the mother's "satisfaction" with herself and the world, all of this mixes unresolvedly, which can sometimes lead to excessive overprotection, but also aggression and abuse towards the disturbed child. However, it should be emphasized that such misguided attitudes on the part of the mother are exceptions. In general, the mother remains bound to her disturbed child with heroic love and care much longer than in normal cases, where the child—quickly and painfully for the mother—moves away from her to follow their own path. However, the disabled child, in whatever way, remains with the mother in the long term. And even though there may sometimes be anomalies in excessively "symbiotic" relationships, in the majority of cases, thanks to the efforts of the parents, especially the mother, the disabled individual has the opportunity to survive and lead a human life far beyond what the state or public institutions could provide, often marked by a cold atmosphere. Certainly, this opens a vast field for counseling and guidance for parents by doctors, psychologists, and social workers.

## Secondary Neuroticization

Due to the harmful educational influences described earlier, as well as the lack of supportive factors, what is termed "secondary neuroticization" occurs. Certainly, this wouldn't go so far if organic brain lesions were not present (because a normally endowed child has a tremendous ability to "overcome" adverse external influences), but the detrimental influence of insufficient education is also undeniable. In this sense, such processes serve as a model for "neuroses" in general: they would not occur without innate or acquired predispositions integrated into the constitution; however, formative influences play a crucial role in their development, and such states are certainly amenable to therapeutic intervention.

As much as disorders cannot be eliminated through medical or clinical treatment, great efforts must be made to prevent or reduce secondary neuroticization, especially through intensive maternal guidance. Precisely because her maternal instinct doesn't help in such cases (the key doesn't fit the lock!), she must intellectually learn to understand the child's abnormal behaviors and respond appropriately.

The doctor is well-suited for this task, as they understand the biological regularities of disorders better - hopefully they can also convey this to the mother! However, they will undoubtedly seek to collaborate within a team where each member, with their knowledge and skills, contributes their part.

## Therapy

Of course, the question arises whether some of the disruptive or even painful behaviors of children with cerebral disorders could be improved with medication. Certainly, modern psychotropic drugs have their place here, especially in cases of extreme agitation. However, the "general effects" of these medications must be taken into account: they not only calm motor agitation but sometimes themselves lead to neurological symptomatology. Most importantly, they can lead to overall inhibition: children appear dull, disinterested; existing concentration problems are often exacerbated, and learning performance diminishes. It should be clear - even though it's sometimes managed this way - that it's not wise to simultaneously administer calming and stimulating medications, which promote impulses. Who could assess the opposing influence of contradictory chemical substances?

Difficulties often arise when children with disorders react paradoxically to a medication, for example, becoming even more agitated with a sedative agent. All of this indicates that the doctor must exercise great caution in drug treatment.

## Educational Treatment

Much can be expected from movement therapy, physiotherapy, especially in cases where motor process disorders are evident (we're not referring here to obvious cerebral motor disorders such as spasticity, athetosis, and others; but attention must be paid to milder symptoms). For these "minor" motor issues (see also the next chapter!), classical methods such as the Bobath method or the Voita method probably won't be used. However, we have observed the benefits of well-directed gymnastics, especially in erethic children who torment themselves and their environment with aimless motor disturbances. If these children can be integrated into a disciplined and joyful group, the teacher is capable of stimulating their enjoyment of movement, commitment, and courage, which represents a significant gain for them. This demands much from the teacher, not only in terms of technical mastery of their methods (assisting precisely where the child needs it to achieve successful experiences), but especially in terms of the ability to individualize, human compassion that captivates and enthuses the child. This is where "curative education" lies in its noblest sense! Other methods can also be used to transform the maladaptive behaviors of children with cerebral disorders into meaningful activities stemming from their own core - musical education (where rhythmically marked music has proven particularly therapeutically effective) - Carl Orff's "schoolwork" has truly pioneered not only for the enjoyment of normal children but also for the treatment of children with disorders. The occupational therapist also has their place on the therapy team: by providing the child with appealing materials, involving them in interesting games, they help them experience success, stimulate creativity, and elevate their behavior to a higher level. Educational guidance is of great importance, particularly for intellectually intact (and therefore more promising) individuals, but it's even more challenging than with individuals suffering from nervous concentration disorders.

## Forms of Organization

All these tasks require effective organization of educational support. Clinical institutions are needed (child psychiatry clinics or educational clinics or units associated with children's clinics, for outpatient or inpatient treatment of children with disorders, these units serving as models for testing therapies and training therapists), a well-structured educational framework, including specialized kindergartens and special schools (including classes for "behavioral disruptors," where the majority of children with cerebral disorders should be directed), and most importantly, something still sorely lacking everywhere today, supplementary training institutions and workshops.

## Further development

This brings us to a painful and often tragic issue: as long as these children are in kindergarten and school, everything goes well for them. They encounter disciplinary difficulties, but the special school teacher is accustomed to this and manages to handle them. The children acquire scholastic knowledge to a completely normal, or even nearly normal extent. Therefore, good prospects for their social future are hoped for - and then heavy disappointment follows! Now they must also succeed in the working world - with an understanding of specific circumstances, perseverance, normal human relationships with colleagues and superiors, with the responsibility for what they are allowed to do and what they are not. We have described above how in people with cerebral disorders, there's often a defect in directing their own activity, from the core of their being, in the form of a "short-circuit," a lack of inhibition, which often leads to dangerous aggression or criminal acts (the next chapter will address "criminality in individuals with disturbed instincts," closely related to the problem present here).

## Ongoing Support

These difficulties that plunge loved ones into despair absolutely require more intensive care and guidance for those now in adolescence. Depending on the type and severity of the disorder, these young individuals will need different types of support: for example, initial vocational training in sheltered workshops, with the prospect of integrating them into independent work situations one day (for instance, organizations like "Jugend am Werk" or "Lebenshilfe"). Sometimes, such a prospect is not feasible, and ongoing support becomes necessary. Such workplaces are available even in rural areas today. To achieve this, contracts must be established with local industries. Despite increasing mechanization, there are still work processes that can only be performed manually, which are relatively well-paid and guarantee at least partial sustainability of the institution. However, it requires creative individuals who can devise appropriate techniques and teach them to those employed here; they experience successful outcomes, take pride in their earned wages, and become socially integrated. If such integration isn't possible because they themselves are too endangered or pose a threat to their environment, long-term institutional placement must be arranged.

## A Digression on Freedom

Curative education, the commitment to disturbed and abnormally reactive children, is a royal path to understanding humanity - to what is assigned to every human being aspiring to knowledge, but especially to all professions dealing with the guidance of human beings. From pathology, one learns to understand - and admire - the "normal" (even though it ultimately remains a mystery). It's precisely when the educator, the adviser to parents tormented by the terrible consequences of short-circuit, uninhibited behavior in individuals with disorders, begins to understand, that one begins to grasp how beautifully organized the activity of a healthy individual is, how they respond to situational demands through their actions, how they are integrated into the human community, integrated into higher bonds and values, capable of free and responsible decisions. Just because the behavior of disturbed individuals is so fundamentally different from that of healthy individuals, this contrasting experience ("ex contrario") constitutes significant evidence of the freedom and responsibility of the mature human, capable of knowing and acting.

Concepts of guilt, repentance, conversion, and tragic failure also take on a new and profound meaning in light of such experiences, just as pedagogical efforts to guide those being led toward their freedom, as well as those in whom it fails but who one wants to protect from harm as best as possible. We believe that such concrete experiences lead further than philosophical deductions.

# V/ DIAGNOSIS OF PERSONALITY DISORDERS IN CHILDREN (1982)

Several methods exist to detect personality disorders in children: a precise and systematic approach including neurological examination of motor skills, electroencephalogram (EEG), pneumoencephalography, psychological tests, and evaluation of sensory functions. These methods will be mentioned often below and have also led to significant advancements in the therapeutic field.

## Diagnostic Approach to Expressive Manifestations

However, it is worth mentioning another avenue of understanding that has proven equally fruitful: a holistic approach that does not rely solely on individually measurable signs but also integrates an intuitive dimension. It's important to note that it's inherent to living organisms to express themselves through external manifestations, to become sensitive, clear, and undeniable, as long as there are organs capable of understanding them. Ludwig Klages laid the foundations for the "science of expression" (the title of his seminal work). Thus, every motor movement carries expression, be it gait (determined down to the smallest genetic details, as shown by twin and family studies), posture (a word imbued with rich relational ambiguity), or even handwriting (a lasting trace of motor action, also scientifically studied by Klages). However, there is an area of motor skills almost exclusively dedicated to expression: facial expressions, which evolved to face forward (rather than downward) and have generally become smooth ("visage," from the Greek "prosopon," turned toward the other, granting it significance). It extremely differentiates all emotions (to the extent that Franz Werfel said, "A smile is not a wrinkle, a smile is the essence of light"; one also thinks of the importance that smiling holds for young children). Visible vegetative manifestations on the outside, in blood vessels (especially on the face, a crucial expressive conduit), and also in glands, are particularly rich in expressive qualities. Intense emotions are visible through manifestations in blood vessels: the pale horror (the fact that simultaneous dryness of the mouth and throat is not directly visible can be identified by swallowing efforts to restore saliva secretion), the "hot" and "red" anger with a congested face taking on a livid hue, distorted grimaces (the gaze also becomes somewhat fixed), eyes "bulging from the sockets" (effect of the vegetative innervation of the eye's protective muscle), wide-open eyelids, increased saliva secretion (drooling). Affective manifestations are accompanied by strong sensations in internal organs, especially the cardiovascular system, but also the gastrointestinal tract. Sensitive children often experience these symptoms very distressingly, and these manifestations can sometimes be visible (for example, when a child experiences extreme fear, the sphincter muscles of the bladder and rectum relax, resulting in "something human" happening to the poor little one, lending an element of tragedy and grotesque comedy). People particularly feel these sensations "at the heart level" - this is not entirely true: it's actually the powerful autonomic ganglionic plexuses surrounding the heart, where so many diverse collective feelings reside. Poets continually describe it. How could they do otherwise, translating it into their language, into images? Thus, "heart and pain" rhyme, and immortal love poems by young Goethe, where heart sentiments play a major role, exist. Interestingly, Homer describes it differently; with him, these collective feelings manifest "en phrên," "at the diaphragm" - but this is also a misconception. It's not the diaphragm muscle, but the celiac plexus below, an important autonomous regulatory center! A child's gaze is the vessel of the richest and most differentiated expression. Describing the precise "instruments" that come into play is still challenging. One could mention: the direction of the eye globe and the interplay of the muscles that move it, the movements of the muscles around the eye, the moistening of the conjunctiva (a "radiant" or conversely "troubled" gaze), the dilation of the pupil. But such indications are meager compared to the emotional richness expressed in a child's gaze (and which poets are also able to describe). Above all, the gaze expresses the nature and extent of interpersonal connections. It's astonishing that the eye, the most important sensory organ through which the world enters a person ("Drink, oh eyes, what the lashes retain from the golden abundance of the world!"), is simultaneously the most important organ of expression, a "mirror of the soul," revealing very clearly what transpires in a child's interpersonal relationships with others: love, trust, or conversely, estrangement, rejection, fear, hostility, hatred (the anomalies in a child's gaze will be extensively described in the chapter on childhood autism).

It is primarily through the gaze that the essential characteristics of expressive manifestations can be understood. When we constantly emit expressions, this happens involuntarily and unconsciously (because it also occurs through vegetative nerve circuits, that is, autonomously); we don't "do" this, but it happens to us, it unfolds within us. This process of expression then corresponds to the impression these manifestations evoke in others, the observer and participant. This impression occurs first unconsciously, as an intuitive, holistic process, not composed of parts (when seeing an angry person, one doesn't sum up the vegetative signs described above, as there probably wouldn't be time to protect oneself from their aggression), but it's grasped in a single "glance," "in ictu oculi." However, those experiencing it are also capable of becoming aware of these processes occurring within them, of recording them. But precisely with this process of intellectualization, possibilities for error also begin. What was infallible as an impression can easily become false when attempting to interpret it. This is where the possibilities for error reside when attempting to judge individuals. Often, after long and bitter experiences, one recognizes that the immediate first impression was correct and subsequent intellectual interpretations led to errors.

### Neuropathy

Expressive manifestations reveal not only the emotions that animate the child in the present moment but also prolonged postures, including anomalies in the adjustments of the autonomic nervous system. A reaction of the autonomic system is often observed, referred to as "vegetative dystonia" or "neuropathy" (we prefer this neutral term as it doesn't provide any indication of etiology, unlike the term "neurosis" which defines manifestations solely based on external situations). The appearance is recognizable, notably through excessive reactions of the skin's blood vessels. Thus, a child can appear terrifyingly pale, to the point where the mother fears a severe anemia.

However, blood tests show entirely normal hemoglobin levels. But the capillaries of the facial skin are under excessive tension ("nervous anemia"). Yet, in a moment of sudden excitement, the face can suddenly turn as red as blood. In these nervous children, other peculiar variations occur in the vessels: sometimes only the ears turn a bright red, or even just one ear! Sweat glands sometimes engage in strange behavior: only the upper part of the nose is covered in large drops of sweat. Trophicity (organ growth) is also vegetatively controlled, and anomalies are found in children with neuropathy: The skin is too thin and "lacking in vitality," for example, around the eyes, the skin lacks so much "resilience" that veins around the eye globe become visible, surrounding the eyes with a dark halo. Such an appearance is always correlated with nervous behavioral disturbances. Thus, these children have truly "written on their faces" and "on their bodies." It's surprising that the nervous nature is not equally reflected in the gaze. There are opposing patterns - as in other aspects: sometimes an especially bright gaze, also indicating heightened emotional excitability (by increased conjunctival moisture). However, there can also be moments of relaxation, or even constant dull and lifeless gazes, revealing the mental emptiness that determines their mode of reaction. Children themselves and their surroundings are often tormented by motor restlessness, particularly intense mimetic agitation. This can lead to facial tics, with undulating and jerky movements on the face; the eyes are particularly restless. But the motor activity of the entire body is also restless: these children fidget and squirm in their chairs (sometimes the chair falls, causing a loud noise at school, disrupting the teacher and the whole class). The movements are so jerky that one might think of chorea, a "choreoid movement" (but the differential diagnosis is easy to establish: if the specific movements in question are strictly interrupted and a targeted movement is requested, like throwing a ball, it is executed in a completely coordinated manner, unlike in minor chorea). We wouldn't have described the physical aspects of the neuropathic state in such detail if they didn't provide clear indications of the psychological symptoms and behavioral disturbances of these children. The "dystonia" of the vegetative system must also manifest on the psychic level, as these functions are what connect and feel with others, allowing the organism to "cling to the world with firmly engaged organs" (Faust). When the vegetative system is imbalanced and tends toward excessive reactions, both psychic harmony and relationships with the environment are disrupted. And so, we find restlessness, irritability, heightened and uncontrollable emotional outbursts, which cause suffering for the children and those around them. Especially lamentable are impairments in work capacity during the school years, and it's at this stage that the described symptomatology reaches its peak (it's better controlled by the developing personality later on). Children are unable to concentrate - a good expression: attention, thought, and work energy must be directed to a center, the goal of the task, while also blocking out all other incoming stimuli; instead, the children seem to "exhaust themselves" (which is clearly visible in their gaze and tone), or they are distracted by everything happening around them ("passive attention"). While they are motivated to perform well in tests that have a strong "incentive character," they fail in the school setting and in task situations, which presents a tragic dilemma for them during decisive years. (Pedagogical methods of concentration will be addressed in another chapter of the book). As a vast experience shows, vegetative peculiarities directly manifesting in expressive manifestations are systematically correlated with behavioral disturbances in neuropathic children. When one learns to "observe" the perceptible manifestations, the nature of these children is revealed, and this knowledge can also have therapeutic implications, both for children with remedial pedagogical methods and for their environment with environmental therapy. For a long time, efforts have been made to distinguish between "functional" disorders (in which functioning is abnormal but there's no indication of anatomically observable lesions) and "organic" disorders, where modifications of the nervous system's substrate can also be identified. This distinction is certainly justified and also holds important consequences. However, one must be aware that in many cases, a clear separation is not possible, as in the realm of living beings in general, there is often neither this nor that, but rather "both this and that." And it must be admitted that it's difficult to conceive that the abnormal vegetative manifestations we've described could occur without "organic" modifications of the nervous substrate; our current investigative methods are simply not refined enough to detect them. Thus, the debate between "organic" and "functional" is ultimately futile, even though the scientist always seeks clear conceptual distinctions and classifications.

Let's now attempt to distinguish organic brain disorders from "neuropathy" (specific disorders will be addressed later in other parts of the work). It can be said that all symptoms are more massive and visible as deficits in normal function; however, they are not always obvious at first glance but reveal themselves through specific examinations. In each individual case, the most important functions must be reviewed, disturbances sought, the effects of a deficit on the entire person understood, and multiple common disorders correctly diagnosed. Let's begin by addressing sensory deficits, particularly in the domain of the visual organ. Major eye anomalies - often caused by embryopathy affecting the organ's formation - are easily recognizable but not amenable to treatment. A much more frequent and highly critical problem is strabismus in children, often neglected and underestimated, yet detrimental (to avoid double images, the child suppresses the retinal image of one eye, leading to strabismic amblyopia, where the child only sees with one eye); treatment is lengthy, requires the use of devices and the involvement of many people, and there are still too few places in the country dedicated to this task. Unfortunately, it's still not a given that upon entering school, or even kindergarten, a sufficiently accurate visual examination is performed by the school physician to detect refraction anomalies, especially myopia; the child who can't see what's written on the board or what's happening on the wall charts suffers defenselessly and lags behind in performance. Yet, the disorder could be completely compensated for with appropriate visual aids! Hearing disorders are even more significant for the children's future prospects. The differential diagnosis: hearing deficit - central language disorder (possibly combined with sensory impairment) - mental retardation - interaction disorder (one who has no relations with other people doesn't "need" language to communicate) is very difficult and requires a lot of experience and a good understanding of childhood peculiarities. Comprehensive examinations must be conducted very early, as soon as the first suspicions arise; because language learning should begin at the same time as the hearing child develops language - during this sensitive phase, the prospects are the best. In early childhood, "play audiometry" is useful (the test must have a strong incentivizing character for the child; the examiner needs good empathy to properly assess the child's reactions); with certain limitations, "computerized audiometry" is also helpful, it assesses brain-evoked potentials based on auditory impressions. Existing auditory residues must be strengthened with hearing aids. Above all, intensive involvement of the mother and speech therapist for infants and school-age children is necessary. But this is truly necessary considering what language represents in human life. Without it, interaction with the world and especially with other people remains at a primitive level; even the normal deaf person almost never learns abstract and conceptual thinking. The tool of human activity is motor function. And it is very prone to disorders due to its long innervation pathways and complex circuits. Especially noteworthy is infantile cerebral palsy, classically described over 100 years ago by John Little with its different forms and named after him: spastic, athetoid, ataxic, atonic. The decisive therapeutic progress of recent years lies in recognizing that treatment outcomes are much better when treatment begins early, meaning in the first months of life, before more severe spasticity develops. Hence, it's essential to quickly screen at-risk children, preferably within a "program for at-risk children," where premature infants and children with a history of difficult pregnancy or birth are called in for thorough examinations and, if necessary, treatment. Several treatment systems exist (Bobath, Vojta), but it's crucial that the mother is trained to become a therapist and is regularly monitored.

It's also important to emphasize that treatment should not be limited to reflex and tone changes through physiotherapy methods, but should encompass the whole child and as many of their functions as possible. Sensitivity should be developed (it forms a "functional circle" with motor skills - and one enhances the other); playing with sand and water has been found beneficial; chewing is particularly trained, not just for eating purposes, but also as a prerequisite for speech; games with different materials offer intellectual stimulation; and finally, those working with children with cerebral palsy are required to possess a special ability to connect - and also charm. What has just been said applies to all curative pedagogy; however, children often reduced in their overall personality level, as described above, require particularly potent pedagogical methods!

For the fate of children with cerebral disorders, it's crucial to determine the extent to which their intellectual functions are impaired. While sensory and motor deficits can be compensated for, or even overcompensated, in individuals with otherwise intact personalities, this is much more challenging in cases of more pronounced intellectual deficits. Therefore, an intelligence test is essential to assess these children, whether the physician has acquired sufficient experience in this field or seeks collaboration with a psychologist.

Of course, the value of the "intelligence quotient" (IQ) is very important. If the IQ is very low, it can't be expected that a critical level of skills will develop, which is essential for meeting life's demands. However, even in children with organic cerebral disorders, there are significant qualitative differences in this domain.

We often see children whose abstract and logical thinking is limited, but some practical life functions are relatively well developed. They are more instinctive than clear-thinking and can handle simple demands. If well-supported by a special school, followed by vocational training and possibly by their spouse later, they can lead an autonomous and fulfilling life. Then, there are completely opposite types: certain intellectual functions are hypertrophied, even beyond the normal range. A grotesque example of this is "memory automatons": they accumulate a plethora of useless information, like all the holidays of the year (we call them "calendar men"), or less useful data like train schedules, phone numbers, bank account numbers, etc. They can then recite all of this like automatons, in a monotone voice, as soon as their memory is triggered. They resemble autistic children (which we'll discuss in a later section), albeit on a much lower level. What they've memorized doesn't assist them in coping with their situation. In reality, they are completely lost in all practical domains and can generally only live in institutions, where they become grotesque characters. But other absurd traits can also be found in children with cerebral disorders: they collect useless objects that they pile up in their rooms, or invent nonsensical machines. To understand such things, one must, of course, take an interest and engage in discussion with them. It would certainly be futile to attempt to take away these characteristics, as it is within these that they find fulfillment in life!

After addressing the intellectual domain, we still need to discuss the physicality of individuals with organic cerebral disorders. Endocrine disorders are not uncommon - this is not surprising, as hypothalamic lesions frequently occur after encephalitis, a region where the "higher command" of endocrine systems takes place. Particularly, there are symptoms clearly linked to a cerebral basis in the case of the pituitary gland, such as growth disorders, but also diabetes insipidus.

Body "trophy" disorders caused by cerebral dysfunctions (proof that all growth processes are directed by the brain) are interesting. Notably, long after early cerebral lesions, it can be observed that the cranial face develops in a unique way. There's hypertrophy of the middle of the face, from the root of the nose downward, affecting the upper and lower jaws; this part is advanced and stubby, sometimes the teeth diverge like in a horse's jaw. The face then strikingly resembles the Neanderthal type (one might wonder: can a cerebral lesion lead to a "primitive rung," a "backward return" to primitive formations already overcome by evolution?). Trophic disorders are also found in individuals with cerebral disorders in other places: finger joints are abnormally stretchable, probably due to joint capsule laxity; sometimes, the terminal phalanges are particularly pointed or, conversely, particularly wide, thus diverging from the norm in a direction.

Such links can be assumed because other signs of organic cerebral disorders are always present. On the other hand, such symptoms serve as an indicator that such a lesion has occurred and can be taken into account for diagnostic purposes. Overall, such observations indicate that the organism is "structured" according to certain developmental laws; once again, pathology is a teacher of physiology, helping us understand what's much more complex in the normal through the pathological.

If indications of epilepsy are identified in the medical history, it is absolutely necessary to conduct an electroencephalogram (EEG).

This is already important because brain seizures can be treated medically.

The multiple behavior disorders due to cerebral lesions will be addressed elsewhere (early exogenous psychopedagogical syndrome). However, at this point, it should be mentioned that if a child's behavior is particularly problematic and hardly influenced by educational means, one should always consider an organic disorder and thoroughly investigate it. It's important for the physician to draw the educator's attention to the presence of such symptoms; otherwise, they risk misinterpreting the behavior and taking misguided approaches in their education, which would be detrimental to the child.


## "Psychopaths", "Character Variants"

Thus, while the physician is obliged to diligently search for signs of organic cerebral causes behind behavioral difficulties, on the other end of the vast spectrum of human possibilities are types of children outside the norm where neurological symptoms are sought in vain, even in the broadest sense. The term "psychopath" was used by early psychiatrists for such types; today, strong reservations are raised against this classification, with which we essentially agree. But in some cases, we also refer to psychopathic behavior. Kurt Schneider, who established a system of such abnormal types, attempted a definition: psychopaths are individuals who suffer from their internal difficulties, and whose environment also suffers from their difficulties. However, this definition is quite vague: it would apply to the vast majority of all possible disorders (including those of cerebral organic origin). This definition of psychopathy also fails to consider the role that the environment plays in the early years of a child's life, causing, maintaining, and amplifying difficulties. Nevertheless, we are also of the opinion that there are innate behaviors (also derived from ancestry) manifesting in all kinds of environmental situations that can indeed be qualified as "psychopathic." An example of this perspective will be described in the section on childhood autism.

How is the diagnosis of such clinical pictures achieved? It starts from the history describing abnormal behaviors, but mostly from contact manifestations and the examination content. Both the information from parents and the child's behavior during interviews and examinations already provide important clues; one "guides" based on this and tailors the subsequent questions according to the child's reactions. Thus, the picture takes shape.

If the child has difficulty speaking, one initially refrains from seeking answers from them and instead offers play material that is so captivating and "stimulating" that they cannot escape it (material developed by the ingenious Maria Montessori is particularly suitable for this age). In this way, as the child gets drawn into the situation, the establishment of contact begins, even if initially inhibited by fear or resistance – and then, the path to verbal contact is not far off!

It goes without saying that one must not give instructions or even reproaches too early. This would block the path of knowledge, as the child would no longer reveal themselves as they truly are; they would become suspicious, withdrawn – or they might start lying to present themselves in a better light. The right path is rather to let the child discover for themselves how they relate to themselves and their situation. If they draw conclusions from this self-understanding, it is much more likely to be profound and enduring than anything imposed or dictated from the outside. However, of course, the adult leading the conversation – whether it be the physician, teacher, psychologist, or social worker – has their opinion and moral stance, and the child must notice this; but they must come to themselves, to make themselves available to the person they have already recognized as trustworthy, someone who must not only be the one who examines coldly but who should feel committed to the child. Thus, (as we've explained in the chapter on medical interviews), diagnosis and therapy, recognizing the child's particularities, and pedagogical-therapeutic conduct should intertwine.

The free interpersonal relationship – as we've described in this section – and precise psychological examination methods, ingeniously developed tests that offer good comparison possibilities through normalization and thus solid diagnostic foundations, should also go hand in hand. Depending on the institution and the personalities working there, it should be decided whether one person manages and uses multiple methods or if a well-coordinated team shares the work but then gathers the results to form a valid picture of the child.

# VI/ MINIMAL BRAIN DISORDERS (1982)

## "Minimal" and "maximal" disorders

Lately, there has been much discussion about disorders that fall within this domain. After lengthy debates about terminology, the term "minimal cerebral palsy" is now being used less often because movement disorders can be so mild that the term "cerebral palsy" is no longer appropriate. Instead, the preference is to use "minimal cerebral dysfunction" or "MCD" as it more clearly expresses the complexity of the disorders with the term "dysfunction." However, the term "minimal" can be misleading. Certainly, motor symptoms can be so subtle that they can only be diagnosed with subtle methods - or even better, with a keen sense of observation of overall motor behavior. But the behavioral disturbances closely linked to them are anything but "minimal"; quite the opposite, they can be maximal, making the children stand out significantly and disruptively within a group, to the extent that sometimes excluding the child from the classroom or kindergarten group seems necessary – and this questions the social future of such a child. Educators, as well as physicians and psychologists, make a serious mistake by not recognizing the organic nature of the disorders. They see the child as "difficult," attempt to address this "difficulty" through disciplinary means which typically remain ineffective, leading to the escalation of repressive measures, and sometimes even abuse when educators lose control. This already illustrates the sometimes tragic seriousness of the situation. Even and especially in this area, assistance must begin with understanding the connections. Although the literature on "MCD" has considerably expanded, it mainly concerns one aspect of the problem, often motor disorders (from the perspective of physicians, pediatricians, or pediatric neurologists) or only the failure of certain mental functions (from the perspective of psychologists). However, here it is important to attempt to see the child as a whole and integrate behavioral disturbances into the overall picture.

## Motor Function

Nevertheless, the observation of motor disorders can guide diagnosis. Therefore, they should be described first. During a thorough neurological examination, anomalies can certainly be found – in muscle tone (increased muscle tone, spasticity, or reduced tone, hypotonia, or even variable tone), in reflexes (for example, in the form of pathological movement patterns, persistence of primitive movement patterns); a significant sign is adiadochokinesia or hypodiadochokinesia (difficulty in speed and skill during rapid forearm pronation and supination); a deformation of the finger known as "bayonet finger" (on extended fingers, hyperextension at the middle joint of the finger, flexion at the distal joint, in any case, a disturbance of finger movement harmony). Asymmetry, one of the described neurological signs, should also be taken into account. However, we believe that it is not just a matter of performing as many reflex tests as possible. Motor disorders can be detected more quickly and reliably by observing complex motor sequences in the child: for example, asking them to demonstrate how to form and throw a snowball; this not only reveals motor disorders but also deficits in action representation (apraxia), and the resulting rocking movement disorder – accompanied by associated psychological symptoms – is also significant. Difficulties in standing or hopping on one foot (especially considering lateral differences), going up or down stairs without stopping, walking on tiptoes or heels, or sitting down (asymmetry, difficulty extending the knee, tendency to tiptoe, inability to touch the tips of the toes with extended knees) show the observer who knows how to "watch" movements many things. Motor function can be variously disrupted in the head region: difficulties in chewing (which can also be identified in the child's early medical history), clumsiness in tongue movements, but especially speech disorders. Given the complexity of innervations, which reflect the integration of numerous brain functions, it is not surprising that even mild cerebral lesions often result in speech motor disturbances. Errors in articulation (incorrect production of certain sounds, especially "s" sounds – sigmatism – or "r" sounds), but also overall poor articulation, unclear pronunciation (making the child's speech difficult to understand); frequent hypersalivation in case of cerebral lesion can also make speech confusing. Stuttering undoubtedly falls within this realm: it is often possible to demonstrate or render very likely that this distressing speech flow disorder has organic cerebral causes – in addition to hereditary factors and in conjunction with "neurotic" factors. The same applies to tics, especially when these involuntary movements are very complex, extensive, leading to more complex events (ringing sounds, but also stereotyped, offensive word formulations, often even coprolalic – thus demonstrating the emergence of dark impulse layers), when the clinical picture evolves into "tic disorders" (Gilles de la Tourette) (it should be noted that, in addition to psychotherapy, drug treatment with neuroleptics also has its chances in such cases). Motor anomalies are generally evident even to non-experts and can therefore serve as diagnostic guides.

## Psychological symptoms

Psychological deficiencies are much more challenging to detect and understand in detail (though they also have repercussions in daily life, especially in the school environment). We should reiterate here what was discussed in the previous chapter on "early exogenous psychological syndrome": the organic disruption of the brain leads – if we attempt to reduce the disruption to a common denominator – to a disintegration of the brain functions that normally constitute the unity of the human person in perception, will, and action. An example of this is the disorder of shape perception, which can also occur with mild cerebral disorders. When we see something, we don't just experience an aggregation of points on the retina as occurs on the retina; thanks to the brain's great integration capacity, a "shape" is revealed to us. However, this capacity can be impaired to varying degrees, as shown by psychological studies (gestalts). Such a disorder can be the cause of learning difficulties, for example, dyslexia (a disorder of the perception of the shape of letters and words). Patient practice, based on understanding the disorder, can certainly bring significant improvement to the child, who is still in the midst of developing their brain functions. It is also clear that perception disorders of this nature can increase the demands of concentration on a student's work to the point of causing them to fail – one of the causes of the often lamented concentration problems in students today. This calls for psychologists and educators working as a team to find ways – with an individual child or, even better, with a group – to improve these difficulties that interfere not only with the academic destiny but also with the life destiny of a child.

## Behavioral Disorders

This brings us to discuss behavioral disorders, which can pose "maximal" challenges in this deviation mistakenly referred to as "minimal cerebral palsy." In most cases, it's not only the inherent disorders in the child resulting from the brain's "dysfunction," but they are further exacerbated by the misunderstanding and inadequate "response" from the child's environment – parents, peers in the social group, and teachers. Thus, a "secondary neurosis" is superimposed in a fatal manner. As extensive as the scientific literature on motor disorders and individual psychological deficits in "MCD" might be, there's little useful information available on treating behavioral disorders (perhaps also because these manifestations aren't easily measurable and can't be statistically captured). In interpersonal relationships, aesthetic qualities undoubtedly play a significant role, even if partners in these relationships might only become consciously aware of this to a lesser extent. However, children in the group addressed in this chapter clearly stand out from what is considered "beautiful" and "pleasant." Even their facial expressions are often different: too immobile, rigid, or even peculiar, not clearly expressing inner emotions – and therefore misunderstood by others, perceived as foreign, or even hostile.

The disturbance becomes even clearer in the realm of motor

skills, especially in smooth motor functions and in more complex activities of childhood. In contrast, we want to describe how a normal child behaves in a concrete situation. The boy enters the classroom with a skipping step, immediately grasping the situation with a quick glance and promptly engaging with his peers. Sometimes, this might escalate into a scuffle among boys, and it certainly serves its purpose in the practice of physical and psychological forces in childhood. It's not unpleasant to watch for the educator; both opponents are skillful enough to avoid serious harm. This absolutely requires a sense of fairness – it's vile, as everyone knows, to seriously endanger the other; and even when one is very angry with the other, they do not cause real harm. In contrast, how wretchedly a boy affected by the disorder we're describing behaves! How stumblingly he presents himself, annoying others to the point that they tease and attack him because they've immediately recognized his clumsiness. The fact that he doesn't dare to throw himself into the fray doesn't help him at all, but only increases the group's aggressions. He can't protect himself, and often something worse happens to him (broken front teeth are a kind of "calling card" for his type). But he can also inflict dangerous harm on the opponent: he doesn't accurately gauge the force of his own blows, and more than his disturbed motor skills bother him, he lacks the previously described sense of a fair struggle with the inhibitions associated with it. In some cases, this is more than just muscular innervation and coordination: from the start, the child has an altered idea of a sequence of actions; they can't implement anything. This is referred to as "apraxia" – and it's precisely this that leaves children so bewildered and powerless in the world. This can be easily verified by assigning the child the task of a complex action, such as forming and throwing a snowball or lighting a candle.

But the attitude of these children towards the authority of the teacher is also severely disturbed. They're seen as terribly bad, disobedient, unruly. Disciplinary measures, punishments, don't lead them to react better; they seem to remain ineffective. It's therefore not uncommon for them to be excluded from class or school, with all the detrimental consequences for their future. But are they truly so unbearably bad? They only get caught so often when they're doing something wrong! The "normal kid," who revels in their mischief and also brings joy to others with it, knows exactly when the teacher will look their way and then puts on an angelic expression, continuing when the watchful eye of the teacher turns away again. However, the boy in our group, who is typically instinctively disturbed, continues and gets caught by the teacher. He's the worst of them all in the teacher's eyes, the one who's incorrigible, unbearable. Such children can also be instigated by others to do anything, without thinking about the consequences, or even without being able to evaluate them. And when this happens, the true mischief-makers gain a double benefit: the teacher is very annoyed, and the incompetent one has fallen into the trap, receiving punishment, which is pleasing to see for the others! This disturbance inevitably makes these children the targets of mockery by their peers. It's entirely incorrect to believe that a mother thinks her boy has had such a hard time in this class, that he's been mistreated here. But if he's transferred to another school, things continue in the same way; because the conflict-ridden situation is inherent to the nature of this child, they magnetically attract the aggressions and taunts of others. It's undeniable that such repeated events deeply influence and traumatize a child. On the other hand, one must understand how challenging psychotherapy is in such a case, as the causes are so firmly rooted in the altered nature of the child due to cerebral disruption.

It should be emphasized that this disorder, which leads to such maladaptation to the real situation, can very well be associated with normal or even higher intelligence. Abstraction abilities, logical thinking, are generally intact in cases of "MCD" (an indicator of this is the fact that in the children's intelligence test "HAWIK" - Hamburg-Wechsler, the "verbal" part of the test, which primarily assesses logical abilities, yields much better results than the "action" part - testing practical skills). However, this often leads to great difficulties in evaluation, for example, by the teacher: one doesn't want to consider behavior as a disorder in a child who can think so well, reason "with sharp clarity" (Morgenstern) (of course, the general truth that logical thinking can go astray if not bound, even merged, with a good perception of reality, with ever-vivid doubts about the reality of thought fantasies, is not taken into account). However, it must be admitted that these disorders not only disrupt class discipline but also the general atmosphere, the "vibe" within a group. Truly to the extreme, such children can be understood as being rejected not only by the teacher but also by their peers (though measures need to be taken in this regard!).


## Instinctive disturbance

This refers to a disruption of these important regulations that initially occur unconsciously and are referred to as "sensitivity," "tactile sensitivity," or even better, "instinct"; they belong to phylogenetic and ontogenetic developmental stages that are older than thought processes. A characteristic of children disturbed on the instinctive level is that they don't know – or lack the sense of – when to speak and when it's better to remain silent. It's said that "thoughts are free"; but someone who is truly anchored in reality certainly doesn't always let these thoughts "manifest in words"; otherwise, they could hurt others and harm themselves! However, these children say what they think without concern, whether it's suitable for the situation or not, whether someone is willing to listen or not, or whether it violates due respect; they also criticize authorities without worry. In reality, this is done with the naivety that characterizes these children. But this particularly disturbs vain individuals and greatly pleases the other children in the group who would never dare to do the same. Once again, a conflict-ridden situation that makes life difficult for this child and others! The attentive reader will have noticed from what has been said that there are similarities with autistic children: difficulties in interpersonal relationships (these could also be referred to as contact disorders), heightened spontaneity without regard for the necessities of the situation, and more or less disrupted expressions. These similarities are so striking that some authors, notably Reinhart Lempp, fundamentally consider autistic behavior as an "exogenous psychological syndrome of early childhood," meaning they believe it's due to an organic brain disorder. We don't subscribe to this opinion. As will be explained in the corresponding chapter, there are certainly children in whom "autism" is "highlighted" by an organic disorder (see page 290); generally, the family history also shows that such behaviors are found in other family members, so one must assume there's a predisposition in this direction, which is certainly "exogenously" realized. However, this is certainly not the case in all instances. Even after a very meticulous examination, there's often no indication of cerebral damage. This thus leads to the necessity of a precise differential diagnosis based on precise neurological examination, especially through "motor diagnostics," by observing movements; it's certain that EEG will also be used, although it must be noted that this examination is often inconclusive, even in cases of organic brain disorder. It's not stated that the prospects of educational and therapeutic intervention depend essentially, or solely, on the presence or absence of an organic disorder. What matters most are the other personality characteristics, especially the degree and specifics of intelligence, the ability to maintain contact, and the other capacities to integrate into the real world.

## Criminality of instinctively disturbed people

The social perspective is sometimes darkened for certain individuals disturbed on the instinctive level when they fall into criminality, committing thefts, frauds, and even usurpations, which have a strangely fantastic quality (and quickly expose them, in contrast to the sophistication of cold and intelligent fraudsters). We must be aware that the capacity to behave socially, to not transgress written and unwritten laws, doesn't solely depend on intellectual understanding of realities (of course, the "understanding of prohibition" plays an important role in the question of "responsibility," both in juvenile and adult justice). But it's not just that: as strong as a child or even an adult may be in wanting to assert selfish desires, even if it encroaches upon the rights of others, normal inhibitions act to prevent antisocial actions.

And this occurs not only because one realizes that punishment will be meted out for doing something prohibited, but also because what happens in the emotional sphere of the decision-maker carries even greater weight: aversion to injustice! Violating the law would be sacrilegious – and sacrilegious action, called "hybris" in Greek, is the central motif of ancient tragedy, which aims to reveal the laws that disrupt the world; this theme runs through the entire intellectual history of the West. And when Goethe says, "Fear is the best part of humanity," he also refers to these feelings that influence our actions. This implies that we are attached to loved ones – parents, teachers, higher authorities – and we don't want to disappoint them; that would hurt them. Finally, we also have emotional relationships with ourselves: the intuition of what we would do to ourselves serves as a powerful warning and protector. The protective mechanisms tragically fail when unfortunate events still occur on the "battlefield of life"; it's despair when later, Goethe's harpist accuses the "celestial powers": "You lead us into life, you let the poor become guilty – then you abandon them to suffering: for all guilt takes revenge on Earth!" But in normal times, these emotional moments are strong enough to prevent unjust actions. The fact that many people fail in this regard is evident in their peculiar behavior after reprehensible acts, a behavior that greatly surprises the judge, the evaluator: the delinquent openly declares what they've done, in the smallest details, even though it's "normal" to lie – at least for children – or at least to deny what one has done.

But here, these "protective mechanisms" fail: when talking to disturbed young individuals, it's as if they don't have the proper relationship with what they themselves have committed – yet they confess it with complete intellectual clarity! (This "objectivity towards oneself," which nonetheless signifies a disturbed self-relationship, we have described as a symptom of autistic behavior). The question of legal responsibility is therefore not so easy to answer. A paragraph (§ 10) of the Austrian Juvenile Justice Act – and correspondingly in other legislations (§ 3 of the German Juvenile Justice Act) – lists two conditions for accountable behavior: "intellectual understanding" and "the capacity to act in accordance with that understanding." The first condition ("understanding") is generally easy to establish, especially through an intelligence test. But it's not easy to definitively determine if someone is capable of acting in accordance with that understanding, especially at the moment of decision and action. Can the "mystery of human actions" truly be completely understood, whether by the actor themselves or even by an external observer? Haven't there always been philosophical schools that question the possibility for the actor to act completely freely? And what about individuals disturbed on the instinctive level, with whom we have observed disturbed relationships with oneself and others? We are convinced that the structure of human orders assumes human freedom and responsibility, that the goal of education in general is to lead young individuals toward this goal, as difficult as it may be. This freedom can certainly be limited or even suppressed in pathological cases (precisely why we consider this, "ex contrario," as an important proof of the "freedom" of the healthy and mature individual!).

Regarding the particular case, it is a challenging task for the observer, such as the adolescent psychiatry expert, to comprehend the individual personality of the accused, to understand their reactions, and to assess the adaptation or non-adaptation of their other actions. In juvenile justice, the question of the maturity of the personality relative to the norm plays a decisive role. The decisive criterion certainly doesn't lie in the ability to prove or disprove brain damage; what seems more crucial to us is to what extent the integration of the personality is intact, to what extent someone can reconcile their understanding with their execution. The precise studies we mentioned show that there are indeed cases where the described instinctual disturbance can be associated with a causal brain lesion. Undoubtedly, this is the most striking behavioral disorder caused by an organic brain impairment. But there are also very similar clinical pictures where it's impossible to prove brain damage.

### Therapy

Finally, let's discuss the therapy for states falling within the medical realm. If one has experience in this field, it's clear that medications can rarely yield results (this can be considered in cases of severe motor restlessness, serious tics; but it must be understood that while reactions can be mitigated to varying degrees, such medications have their "side effects" – the pharmaceutical industry speaks too euphemistically – and this can often lead to a general decrease, for example, disruption of concentration and attention at work; thus, the desired effects must always be weighed against possible harms!). Psychotherapy that seeks to explore these complexes and influence their dynamics has little chance of success – it can only be effective in the sense that, in "family therapy," parents are guided to avoid "secondary neuroses." Undoubtedly, the most important treatment falls within the realm of therapeutic education. A significant part of this involves understanding that the child suffers from a brain-originated disorder rather than deliberate malice: when they don't exert effort during physical exercises, it's not that they're lazy, but rather they don't meet the legitimate demands imposed on others; the child who doesn't keep their notebooks clean, scribbles, or doesn't practice reading sufficiently isn't lazy, and they react to this in various ways, whether through withdrawal, closing up, or even depression, or indeed through malice, opposition, or even aggression (which can become dangerous precisely due to their awkwardness): their difference, as well as their clumsiness, incites others to attack them – and everything worsens more and more! And of course, the instinctual blunders described above also provoke hostility from classmates and especially the teacher towards this child. This leads to constant suffering for the child when the teacher, lacking understanding, succumbs to their emotions and consistently resorts to increasingly severe punitive measures, leaving the child defenseless. In such cases, the school physician, if they've developed an eye for such peculiarities, is the child's natural advocate. They must introduce the teacher to concrete realities and motivate them to assist the child in turn – and the first important step is understanding. The educator understands that a child's behavioral difficulties stem not from lack of will or malicious intent, but from a disorder, so they approach them completely differently: with empathy, even sympathy, they spare them instead of punishing, they reduce the demands placed on the child according to their abilities, preferably in a way that the child doesn't even notice, thus offering them the opportunity to succeed, which in turn serves as powerful motivation for the child. They'll seek to discover the positive aspects that persist despite the disorder, sometimes even exceptionally, such as in the intellectual domain; because here too, there are "overcompensations," as Alfred Adler brilliantly described: in cases of "organic deficiency," there are opportunities to not only compensate for deficits but even achieve exceptional things; it's as if the defects awaken forces that aren't at the disposal of the "norm." We have drawn comparisons with autistic behaviors – indeed, in the treated group of children, one often observes a strong spontaneity and originality of thought. However, the teacher must certainly consider these child's peculiarities, recognize them, and encourage them. Thus, they prepare a much more favorable ground for the child's growth and development. Among the important tasks of the educator of such children is also influencing the group in favor of the child. We previously described the "natural" difficulties between them and their social group. But one cannot simply let things proceed as such, for this would result in damage on both sides. Of course, it's not easy to change this for the better, and it doesn't happen quickly. However, one can foster a better atmosphere in the group by showing what this "ugly duckling" (H. Ch. Andersen) is capable of, the efforts they make to cope with their disorder. Thus, a good teacher can truly create an atmosphere of benevolence towards such a child. Of course, it will often be necessary to remove the child from dangerous situations – for example, sending them on an errand during recess or even protecting them from the group's aggression on the way to school. As important as understanding towards a child with brain disorders is, many actions must be taken to improve their condition. This primarily concerns the domain of motor skills, in which they are mostly delayed.

While a normal child interacts with their environment through their motor apparatus, which obediently responds to them without effort with a good "pleasure of functioning" (Ch. Bühler), a child with disorders in this domain requires stronger stimuli, they need assistance both for gross motor skills (especially movement) and fine motor skills. And of course, it's essential to detect and treat the disorder as early as possible (ideally from early childhood). At any age, this requires heightened personal attention, it also requires the charm of the physiotherapist as well as strong "motivational character" for the required exercises.

The younger the child is, the more we will seek to involve the mother as a "co-therapist": at an early age, she is the one who transmits the child's environment to them, with reason and emotion. Of course, this requires constant guidance and supervision from a qualified physiotherapist. As much as the mother is advantaged by her ability to establish contact with the child, one must combat in her an erroneous attitude called "overprotection": the mother who notices her child's delay compared to normal behaviors early on is overwhelmed with compassion and tries to eliminate all obstacles for her precious disabled child, making daily tasks that could challenge their abilities easier for them, instead of taking the necessary time and patience to assist them just enough so that the child doesn't become discouraged, but still giving them enough autonomy.

Particular weight must be given to the stimulation of oral motor skills. Even children slightly affected by brain disorders don't spend enough time chewing and reject solid foods, preferring to continue using their bottle. This poses nutrition problems, as the growing child's body also needs fiber-rich and solid foods. It's also important to note that correct mouth and tongue movements are a prerequisite for speech. Therefore, it's essential to stimulate the child in this area by creating the right conditions for muscular tone (head and trunk control) and teaching them good habits of jaw, mouth, and tongue movement through appropriate techniques.

Later on, in addition to individual stimulation, group movement therapy can be considered, with all the stimuli it involves: competition, achievements in comparison to others, harmonization in a positive common atmosphere (of course, the educational group leader must be able to precisely personalize in order to avoid frustrating experiences for the child). The assistance provided by the teacher must be applied at the right time and in the right place – this way, the child gains confidence in their own abilities and becomes a full-fledged member of the group.

Specific disorders such as shape perception problems or the well-known dyslexia require specific aid methods, which have been recently developed from a psychological standpoint. The same can be said for concentration problems in work, an issue that today goes beyond the simple medical realm and widely concerns the "norm": working distractedly at school and during homework has become an almost ubiquitous difficulty, thus becoming a general task of learning management. According to our opinion, it's about avoiding soulless mechanical exercises and "engaging" children with personal investment, facing them with eye contact and speech, offering them methods that fascinate them and immerse them in a productive atmosphere. There are good tools available today that captivate children.

Treating concentration problems in children – once again, not only in cases of medical issues – justifies all efforts: the disorder is "typical for the phase" (unless it's extreme forms in a child with organic brain disorders), and based on our experience, it peaks towards the end of primary school; however, in adolescence, when the young individual reaches a new stage of awareness and gains better self-control, this disorder naturally decreases and young individuals learn to work. However, if they only experience failures at school as long as they cannot yet learn in a concentrated manner, thus losing the chance to attend higher education, their social future is seriously threatened. Therefore, it's necessary to assist them during this critical period.

We express our conviction that even children with medical disorders have developmental potential, and here too, the physician is "time as an ally." This disorder is perfectly compatible with good, even above-average intelligence, which obviously improves the prognosis. One must understand these children, sometimes protect them within their social group, provide them with help – and in most cases, all of this offers good prospects.

# VII/ THE PSYCHOLOGICALLY ABNORMAL CHILD (1938)

We are in the midst of a profound transformation of our intellectual life that has affected all areas of this life, especially medicine. The key concept of the new order – that the whole is more important than the part, and the people are more important than the individual – has had to bring about deep changes in our attitude here, where it concerns the most precious good of the nation, its health.

It is not my intention to discuss here in detail the specific changes in the particular field of childhood psychopathology. You are aware of the means by which we seek to prevent the transmission of a diseased genetic heritage – in many cases, it involves hereditary disorders – and promote genetic health. As physicians, we must fully assume the responsibilities that fall to us in this area.

However, today, allow me to not approach the problem from the standpoint of the entire nation – which would lead us to primarily discuss the law on the prevention of procreation by subjects with hereditary diseases – but from the perspective of abnormal children. The question is what we can do for these individuals. And when we help them with all our dedication, we also render the best service to our nation – not only by preventing these individuals from burdening the national community with their antisocial and criminal acts, but also by seeking to help them find their place as workers within the living organism of the nation.

To begin, it seems necessary to define a concept: anything that deviates from the ordinary, therefore "abnormal," should not necessarily be considered "inferior" as a result.

A case will serve as an example to explain this assertion, which may appear contradictory at first glance.

A ten-year-old boy presents himself at our clinic; he is in the first year of middle school. His father reports serious difficulties. At the forefront is his sensitivity, not only at the level of bodily sensations (in various sensory domains), but particularly his psychological sensitivity. A few examples: he has always had great difficulties with food; he doesn't like any of the common dishes, but he is passionately fond of very acidic foods (this trait is, incidentally, frequent among psychopathic children); he has trouble falling asleep, especially if he is restless or has eaten shortly before bedtime; he generally has a light sleep. He is highly anxious and uncertain, fearing for his health in all circumstances. He takes the smallest details to heart and is sometimes, as he puts it himself, "all melancholic." But the most serious conflicts arise from his psychological sensitivity, from his irritability: small events provoke scenes where he behaves "like a madman." Therefore, the father wonders if the boy is psychologically normal.

Overall, the boy presents many "abnormal" aspects. His behavior is in line with what has been described. Although he maintains a certain appearance, appearing very self-assured, sometimes even "dominant," it quickly becomes evident how much insecurity and fear hide behind this forced confidence. In reality, in only slightly extraordinary situations, he is constantly on the brink of losing control; one senses that with a slightly stronger demand, he will tip over, resulting in a strong explosion of excitement.

However, the boy has another aspect that – on the surface – is in strange contradiction with the described abnormal symptoms: he is incredibly intelligent for his age. This is manifested notably in his language, which fully corresponds to that of an educated adult due to its complex sentence structure and selected vocabulary. But his areas of interest are also those of an adult. He ponders religious and philosophical questions, observes people with genuine psychological interest, and has insightful observations about their particularities, especially their weaknesses. It's evident that he is always the best in his class; his school essays provoke "sensations"; he doesn't make spelling mistakes, and he easily passed the entrance exam to middle school.

In summary, on the diagnostic level: he is an intellectually gifted boy, finely differentiated character-wise, sensitive, with many physical and psychological sensitivities.

How should we approach the portrait of this personality? Is it a fortuitous coincidence of abnormal traits and exceptional qualities? Or should we analyze this case according to the schema of individual psychology: to escape the inferiority of different organic systems and the very damaging feelings of inferiority that result, he might have taken the path of overcompensation of these inferiorities with exceptional intellectual achievements; thus, inferiority would be the cause of superiority (as suggested by the example of individual psychologists, according to whom Demosthenes owed his greatness as an orator to his stuttering, as it motivated him to succeed!).

We believe neither one nor the other. We affirm – not based on theory, but from the experience of many children – that the positive and negative traits of this boy are two naturally linked aspects of a completely coherent personality. This can also be expressed as follows: the difficulties this boy faces within himself and in his relations with the world are the price he must pay for his particular talent. What distinguishes him particularly is also particularly vulnerable. We must imagine: this individual possesses more sensitive sensory organs, a finely differentiated brain. However, he is also more sensitive, more easily hurt and damaged by influences from his environment. Those who know children will constantly find examples showing that gifted but less childlike children must pay for their wealth with specific internal difficulties, including psychopathic traits.

We also find parallels to what we have said in the field of brain disorders: it is an empirical fact that tuberculous meningitis particularly often affects exceptionally intelligent children, intellectually advanced beyond their age, and finely differentiated in character, and carries them away. "He was too good for this world," parents often say. When we say that his brain was vulnerable to external insult precisely because it was too refined an instrument, that's essentially saying the same thing. Or take another example: this year, we had the opportunity to observe two identical twin sisters who simultaneously developed hemichorea. The sisters were, as expected for identical twins, not only physically, but also characteristically very similar. However, they exhibited very marked differences in their personality structure: one was more primitive, coarser, more carefree, less interested, less intelligent, while the other was noticeably more intelligent, more mature, and richer emotionally. The second sister not only had much more serious illnesses than the other, but she also had a much more severe, longer-lasting chorea, accompanied by more serious psychic symptoms. Not a coincidence, we are convinced; the more finely organized brain was more vulnerable to the chorea virus, as we could see with exemplary clarity in this case, where we could assume with absolute certainty that the environment and dispositions were the same for both twins, except for the mentioned character difference.

The described facts show us that "abnormal" symptoms can be an integral part of the portrait of a personality, inseparable from its positive aspects. Good and bad within a person, their strengths and failures, their possibilities and dangers are drawn from the same sources and mutually conditioned. We won't delve into the conclusions that can be drawn from such knowledge for psychology as a whole here, but we will only discuss therapeutic conclusions. Given what has been said, we will understand that it is often not possible, or even desirable, to eliminate troubling symptoms through treatment, although we can also achieve much here (which will be discussed later when suggestive therapy is addressed). Furthermore, our therapeutic goal must be – a goal that can be achieved in psychologically differentiated individuals, even in children – to teach individuals to bear their difficulties rather than eliminate them, to educate them to transform their particular difficulties into exceptional accomplishments, and to make them aware that they are not sick, but responsible. It's not enough to explain the connections to children once and for all, but it's also important to emphasize that continuous, timely action on the part of the educator must accustom the child to increasing demands.

Also for the second child I want to discuss before you, it's a contrast between pathological character traits and, in a certain way, great value; but here, we must talk about a profound personality disorder. The 7½-year-old boy has posed serious educational problems since early childhood. He doesn't submit to any foreign will and takes malicious pleasure in not obeying and annoying other people. Even the school can't control him; he disrupts the entire class with his teasing and fighting; if he weren't such a good learner, he would have already been expelled from school. Here again, it concerns a psychopathic personality, whose abnormal behavior manifests primarily in the form of educational problems. Once more, we want to find the key to his personality from precise knowledge of his behavior, and the right educational behavior from knowledge of the personality. Children of this psychopathic type, to which the presented boy belongs, often match not only in character but also in body structure and even in their movements down to the smallest details. We have before us a massive, coarse, and unrefined boy who looks older than he is. Even in the few movements you have been able to observe in him, his blatant clumsiness is evident (it's significant that the big boy still has to be dressed by his mother; even in his hastily written, slow-paced handwriting, his complete awkwardness is evident).

## Behavior

The educator encounters severe disciplinary difficulties here – I want to emphasize that this is in an excellent educational environment where people are accustomed to easily managing difficulties primarily caused by exogenous influences (spoiling or other unfavorable family environment). The boy does many things; he's incredibly mean to other children, some see him as a troublemaker. He seems almost impervious to educational influence. Sometimes it's thought that he's deaf, but he's simply "disabled"; he disregards educational influences just as he remains unaware of so many things in the world. And that's also the essence of his disorder: his relationships with the world are limited, especially those that don't play out through intellectual understanding but through instinctive comprehension. Let's realize how children, especially young children, are educated: they integrate into the world and maintain normal relationships with it, not because they consciously understand the content of the educator's instructions (they've already been educated well before being capable), but because they instinctively feel attached to the educator, because they instinctively understand what's conveyed by the tone of words, by the educator's facial expressions and gestures, and because they respond correctly to his behavior with their own behavior, having been instructed through countless unpleasant and pleasant experiences. This instinctive understanding is now severely disturbed in these children. All abnormal symptoms stem from the disturbance of instinctual functions: disturbance of situational comprehension and disturbance of relations with others; from there, we understand the lack of respect for authority, in general, the lack of disciplinary understanding; but we also understand the fact that these individuals are not liked by anyone, we understand the senseless meanness. To this absence of instinct is added not only clumsiness in purely motor domains but also practical misunderstanding, difficulty in achieving learning success, "difficulty in mechanization." The fact that these children are always loners, finding themselves outside every group of children, is not surprising given what's been said: they seek no community within themselves because they have no personal relationships with anyone (they never have friends), and the community itself rejects them because they're always an alien entity; however, they're always the object of unanimous ridicule by the community due to their peculiarities, especially their clumsiness, for which they often know how to take revenge.

In such severely restricted personalities, as with this boy, one thing is often not only undisturbed but even exceptionally well developed, namely, intelligence in the strict sense, the ability to think logically, to formulate thoughts linguistically correctly (they often come up with particularly original, even language-creative expressions); there are often surprisingly mature special interests, often genuinely scientific (such as natural research) or technical interests, which are often again quite eccentric, strange, and marginal. A very characteristic symptom we can also observe in this boy is "objectivity towards his own meanness": these children can perfectly describe how mean they are; they voluntarily add new interesting features to their character profile when you talk about it. One might think that if a child knows so well how mean he is, if he seems to understand all of this so clearly, he should be very easy to educate. But that's a big mistake that many educational counselors fall into. The opposite is true. A "normal kid" either can't talk about their meanness because they're not conscious of it, or they refrain from telling an adult, thus giving them ammunition. But when a child talks about their nonsense so freely and unaffectedly, you can be sure that they can only be pedagogically influenced in a limited way. Scholastic knowledge is also generally very characteristic in these children: where logical thinking is required, where the subject corresponds to their particular interests, they excel, stunning the teacher with their intelligent answers; but where it comes to learning more or less mechanically, where concentrated work is required (copying, spelling, calculation methods), these "smart" children fail flagrantly, often coming close to failure.

Within this well-characterized group of children we call "autistic psychopaths" due to their restriction of relations with the external world, their focus on the self (αὐτός), there are, of course, different individuals who must also be evaluated differently. Sometimes the originality of thought (which always includes a certain "autism") or the intensity of particular interests, which seem hypertrophied at the expense of many other skills, is so emphasized that such individuals are capable of exceptional performance (who doesn't know the autistic researcher, who has become a comedic figure due to his clumsiness and lack of instinct, but who can achieve remarkable things, even advancing his often very narrow specialized field!). Other times, autistic originality only appears as aberrant, eccentric, and useless (the fact that a thought is perceived as strange and singular can be due either to the fact that it points towards the future and will later become a living reality or to the fact that it has nothing to do with reality). In this latter case of autistic psychopaths, the disruption of adaptation to the environment, the inability to learn, is emphasized and unfavorably determines the social prognosis. There are fluid transitions between these states of severely disturbed personality and schizophrenia, of which the essential symptom is also autism, the loss of all contact with the environment. The relationship of such patterns with schizophrenia is also evident in the fact that not only singular autistic individuals but also genuine schizophrenics are often present in the families of these individuals.

The boy presented, like many children of this type, is an only child. We cannot make a remark about this, as it seems to lead us to a deeper understanding of these cases. The school of individual psychology would explain all the disturbances this child presents by the "only child situation," by the lack of independence, and the "consequence" of clumsiness, by the child's intellectual maturity from "growing up among adults," etc. All of this would thus be exogenous damage. We claim rather that the fact that the boy is an only child is somehow linked to his constitution, to his genetic heritage! The mother of this boy is characteristically very similar to her son: she's entirely intellectual, eccentric in her nature, has little emotional connection with her child. The fact that this woman, along with her son in this case, transmitted this psychopathic disposition to her son and doesn't show maternal warmth, refusing to endure the pains and inconveniences of multiple pregnancies, the difficulties of raising multiple children, is evident. This is as well-founded in her nature as the boy's difficulties are in his. Thus, we often see that things that at first seem conditioned by the environment are actually determined by inheritance or are at least greatly influenced by it.

## Pedagogical Implications

You will understand from what has been said how difficult it is to educate such children. They lack, in a way, the organ that facilitates their education. If the situation isn't hopeless, it's because there's something to address in them, namely, their intelligence. Precisely what instinct-lacking educators normally do with normal children, namely, explaining and justifying educational requirements, is here the only path to follow. For the usual method, in which the educator acts primarily through their personality, in which it matters how they say something, not what they say, in which their "expression" (voice, facial expression, and gesture) becomes increasingly penetrating and affectionate in case of resistance from the child, until, as a last resort, a "saintly thunderbolt" certainly achieves the desired goal – all of this doesn't impress these autistic children at all; it's an interesting sensation for them that they enjoy with mischievous joy and even deliberately provoke ("I'm happy when my mother bangs the table," the boy being presented says with mischievous eyes). On the other hand, these children can become aware of the "rules of behavior" that are given to them and fulfill them – like a mathematical equation, for example. The more "objective" such a law is, for example in the form of a schedule covering all possibilities of the day and to be adhered to meticulously on both sides, the better. In this way, and not through an unconscious and self-developing instinctive habit, it's possible to achieve, over the years, through laborious and conflict-ridden work, the best possible adaptation to the community, which succeeds better and better with increasing intellectual development.

In the foregoing, I have described a type whose fundamental abnormality stems from a disharmony between intellect and instinct, in the sense of a disorder of instinct. In child psychopathology, there's also a type that represents almost all aspects opposed to what has just been described: these children have below-average intellectual development (down to mental retardation), where intelligence is understood as abstract intelligence, while practical intelligence, in short, everything related to instinct, and therefore practical usefulness, but also emotional values, are relatively better developed. These latter cases are important, or will become important for us when the "Law for the Prevention of Progeny Afflicted with Hereditary Diseases" also comes into effect. When a physician is called to act as an expert in such cases, they cannot make a decision solely based on the result of a questionnaire or the number of the intelligence quotient but primarily based on their knowledge of the child's personality, a knowledge that takes into account all of the child's capacities, and not just abstract intelligence.

The purpose of a short exposition can obviously not be to provide a systematic overview of child psychopathology. It seemed preferable to me to choose two not too severe but promising cases, in order to show the course of our therapeutic action. This course starts with the knowledge of the child's personality, the experience of educational difficulties, the direct experience of abnormal reactions, to arrive at the educational action adapted to the child's particular nature, which maximizes their precious innate abilities and neutralizes as much as possible the dangers inherent in them. This last sentence actually expresses the goal of all education; only, the path is more difficult for individuals who don't fit the norm; it requires experience, even love for these children, and the educator's complete commitment of personality.

Even in such a brief exposition, we must address a method of treating psychological disorders that, upon careful reflection, is the primary method not only in the field of psychotherapy but also the primary method in medicine in general. Today, we know once again (this knowledge has been temporarily overshadowed, mainly due to the rise of scientific healing methods and their successes) that for successful treatment even of seemingly purely organic diseases, in addition to chemical and physical treatments, the physician's personality must also come into play. To a considerably greater, even decisive, extent, this must also apply to the treatment of "functional" disorders – I refer here to various organic neuroses such as functional vomiting and coughing, pains in different organs, enuresis, sleep disturbances, anorexia, as well as psychic symptoms like heightened excitability or states of anxiety. The essential element of the healing mechanism is as follows: the powerful personality of the physician leads the patient to turn away from their pathological symptoms, regardless of their underlying cause, regardless of the origin of their disturbed personality. What ultimately brings about healing is the patient's trust in the physician's healing capacity; this trust brings about a curative adjustment of the nervous system.

We call this type of treatment suggestive therapy. In a broader sense, the entire behavior of a good educator is also suggestive treatment: their powerful personality compels the child to follow the right path. Thus, we now know that appropriate educational behaviors can significantly contribute to the maintenance or restoration of a child's nervous health. We have long known that many nervous disorders, which can also manifest as physical illnesses, can be "cured" by the correct and confident behavior of entirely ordinary people, for example, nurses, even without them being aware of their influence. So, this is also a "suggestive therapy."

The physician is particularly well-placed in this situation. Trust in their healing capacity is readily granted from the outset; of course, to achieve success, they must also possess the corresponding personal prerequisites. Particularly due to the work and actions of Hamburger, the following method has proven very favorable: the physician prescribes a medicine (obviously neutral) or a procedure, acting as if treating an organic condition. In reality, this medicine, this procedure, is the visible sign, the material basis to which not only the patient but also their surroundings entrust themselves (this latter point is particularly important when treating children: the trust that the surroundings, especially intermediaries, show throughout the day, expressed in all their behavior, is the most potent support). It's precisely through this that an automatic curative adjustment of the organism occurs (Hamburger's thymogenic automatism), due to its influence on the forces of the spirit (θυμός) – Hamburger terms all such treatments "thymotropic."

The brevity of time does not allow for the presentation of several cases that would demonstrate how the treatment method must adapt to the peculiarities of each disorder, how the remedy is decreased, increased, or changed based on success or failure. One last thing should be said: even in highly abnormal individuals, suggestive treatment of particularly distressing symptoms is promising. The realization that these individuals are afflicted with a primary constitutional or even hereditary impairment should by no means lead to the conclusion that nothing can be done – just as the recognition of endogenous disorders should not lead to educational nihilism. The education of abnormal individuals is also promising, not only because environmental influences, like good education, are very important (they can bring out the good in predispositions, prevent further harm – how important it is, for example, to avoid conflicts in those with very high excitability!) – the fact that we must never outright abandon the education of abnormal individuals as hopeless is also due to the fact that with these individuals, forces and abilities may suddenly emerge in adolescence, for example, that were certainly predisposed but of which we had no inkling in childhood, and it was impossible to predict that they would become so significant.

The physician has the right and duty, I hope I have shown you in a few words, to be an educator, not only an educator for the community with a view to healthy living, but also to decisively influence the education of abnormal individuals. They must be capable of giving advice and aid based on their clear insight into the interactions of nature, on their understanding, and thereby serve not only the individual but also the nation.

# VIII/ CHILD ANTISOCIALITY: LIES, THEFT, RUNAWAYS (1982)

## The path to socialization

Everything discussed in this work is guided by the biology of the child, by their normal or pathological developmental processes. This also applies to this chapter. Normally, the young child is entirely egocentric, shamelessly seeking to satisfy their impulses, first by crying, and then, once their motor functions have matured, by extending their activities widely. The path a child must traverse to become a member of the human community is very laborious. If the human being, according to Aristotle, is a living being that forms communities, they are not born as such but develop gradually and laboriously into one, shaped by the authority of their environment. Therefore, from a biological standpoint, it is absurd when Alexander Neill declares in his once-famous book "Summerhill: A Radical Approach to Child Rearing" that authority should be replaced by freedom in education. But how can a child truly be "free" when they haven't yet developed their inhibitory mechanisms and lack sufficient experience? For a human being who is in no way supported by instinctive regulations, it would be cruel to push them prematurely into an apparent freedom. Education, more transmitted through lived authority than preached authority, is for them a biological necessity! The common goal of socialization is to engage with others, to consider their well-being, and to suppress selfish desires. Certainly, an important motive is a form of higher altruism: one is rewarded by receiving more than they give, exchanging the respect and love of others for what is initially denied. Let's take an example. What happens, we ask, in a two- or three-year-old child when they and their mother succeed in toilet training? We can believe Sigmund Freud when he says that the uncontrolled emission of stool and urine is associated with pleasurable sensations for the very young child. However, when the child learns to control these functions – and gives up this primitive pleasure – they exchange their mother's love, respect, and pride for this self-denial and are thus rewarded at a higher level. The pursuit of love – or the fear of maternal love deprivation – guides the child onto the path of obedience. My teacher F. Hamburger made a very relevant distinction between obedience to prohibition, which appears much earlier, even in infancy, and obedience to commands, which requires a more advanced capacity for understanding. Thus, under normal conditions, the child grows up within an order of life, experiencing both good and bad and conforming to it. They learn that human connections entail responsibilities, that others' property must be respected, and that honor must be given to the truth. This learning process requires both internal maturation processes (the capacity to inhibit primitive impulses and the accumulation of "engrams" in the central nervous system) and work done by educators, particularly by the mother. If this does not occur, the phenomenon of neglect becomes apparent. It is interesting to examine the origin of this word, which comes from the ancient language: "diu wäre" means "protection, guardianship" against misfortune; the prefix "ver-" means the opposite, "deprived of protection." Whoever is deprived of protection against misfortune is precisely abandoned to their fate. Here as well, it is verified that education must take place "at the right time," during this "sensitive phase" of early childhood, which should not be neglected as such neglect is difficult to rectify later on. The impressive studies by Bowlby and René Spitz on "early deprivation" attest to this.

## Infantilism

What then causes antisocial behavior, an inability to conform to social norms? First and foremost, it is worth mentioning maturation delay, infantilism. Infantile individuals are often structured by their defect in a way that makes their abnormality easily recognizable: their proportions, both large and small (such as the face and skull), remain childlike for a long time, their dentition is delayed; their facial expressions are too "open"; the child hasn't yet learned to establish distance – and this is clearly noticeable in their psychomotor skills: particularly their gaze shows that the child cannot maintain distance from others, they illuminate them with their presence, adapting too easily to everything, being entirely "open to the world" (Wilfried Zeller described this well – he contrasts how the distance, the critique of the obvious, which is a characteristic trait of school and professional maturity, can already manifest in a child's gaze, an important trait for those experienced in this field). Similarly, such an immature child immediately and without hesitation seizes whatever is within their reach and tries to claim it, thus violating others' property rights. There are numerous possibilities: from "scraps" akin to a magpie's collection of useful and useless things that vanish into the mysterious pockets of a boy, to seemingly well-thought-out thefts where all obstacles are skillfully overcome, opportunities are identified and exploited.

## Cerebral Disorders

If some individuals, due to their constitution, are predisposed to antisocial behaviors, individuals with cerebral disorders face even greater, often insurmountable, difficulties in socializing. We should refer to what has been discussed in the chapters "Exogenous Psychological Syndrome of Early Childhood" and "Minimal Brain Damage" regarding the activity disorders of these children. We spoke of a "misalignment": at the moment of decision-making, experiences, higher evaluations, necessary inhibitions do not intervene properly, actions occur in a "short-circuited" manner, leading to severe consequences, despite sometimes genuine intellectual understanding, despite genuine remorse after the act. We have also described the poor prognosis for these personality disorders. Those who are delayed in their maturation, the infantile individuals, and those with cerebral disorders are two types of people who seem particularly predisposed to sinking into asocial behavior. Now, we must discuss environmental factors and their interference with personality traits that hinder socialization.


## Theft

As one of the many causes of theft in children, we first mention the modern consumer mentality, which is constantly instilled in children by mass media, especially television (advertising psychology employs sophisticated means, and children are completely defenseless against it). However, this often results in conditioning children towards property offenses. Parents who themselves are under the influence of this mentality must be aware – and take appropriate precautions – that they themselves are complicit when children appropriate things that do not belong to them, driven by excessive greed. Of course, there are degrees of seriousness in theft, in the assessment of adults and the awareness of children. It is not considered as severe if a child takes money from their father or mother's wallet: "What belongs to the parents also belongs to me!" It's even worse when a child steals from classmates, and worse yet when they steal from strangers. Theft in large stores presents a particular "gray area": the term "self-service store" then takes on a grim double meaning – everything seems to be there, very tempting, ready to be taken; sometimes, children are driven by a sportive ambition to succeed with their skills. There's often competition among those similar, an element that suppresses inhibitions, and there's also clever cooperation between the perpetrator and the observer, also in a "noble" competition. Damages can be significant, the habit of stealing, which can lead to genuine addiction, plays a crucial role: theft becomes a pleasure. In older individuals who already possess a certain critical distance from the world, a sense of triumph may arise towards a worldview that considers possession and enjoyment as the greatest of goods (regardless of the clarity or obscurity of this in a child's experience).

## Serial delinquency

In this context, we consider the following observation to be important, for children, adolescents, and adults alike: series of thefts tend to continue until there is a discovery, a catastrophe. The culprit is then reproached (even by the prosecutor, if the case goes to court): it is particularly blameworthy to continuously carry on with the series of offenses instead of stopping on one's own. However, this is not humanly understandable. Such series continue almost automatically according to an internal logic; it's only when the discovery illuminates the entire dark sequence of events like a flash of lightning that genuine reflection, a "catharsis," a purification can take place.

Indeed, everything that follows such an event can offer: discovery, legal proceedings, confrontation with individuals and norms, important impulses for personality development. It's so important that poets have often addressed it in their human portrayals, especially in their autobiographies, like Gottfried Keller in "The Young Henry" or Thomas Mann in several of his works. This way, the inevitability of these experiences throughout a lifetime is highlighted, better than what could be achieved in scientific debates.

## Prediction

This brings us to the question of predicting such antisocial activities in children. Based on our experience, in cases where none of the personality anomalies described above are present, the prognosis is generally favorable; parents' concerns that their children who have already stolen might have a criminal future usually do not materialize! Physiologically, the understanding and the ability to make decisions based on this understanding develop in young individuals and eventually ensure social adaptation, behaving in accordance with community requirements.

However, it must be acknowledged that this "cultural layer" that is supposed to develop in individuals on phylogenetic and ontogenetic levels is not very stable: in extreme situations, during times of war and revolution, in times of great distress, even in adults, there's no concept of property; only a few escape the attraction to cast aside moral orders! It's also worth mentioning that the majority of people – when asked decades later about what they did when they were children – have completely forgotten these things.

## Truth and Lie

The other part of this chapter, the issue of truth and lying, must also be considered from the perspective of developmental biology if one wants to follow the reality of the child.

If a child, between the ages of two and four, has learned to "master" language, they are also aware of the power this grants them: according to the biblical narrative, Adam gained control of the world by giving names to the things around him, by giving them words! Language has a life of its own in the child: what develops in terms of ideas and desires within them is not strictly separated from what adults call reality. For them, imagination is entirely real. It's in fairy tales, it's in the role-playing of the early years of childhood that they feel "at home," without making any distinction or separation from reality. There's no doubt that this "illusionistic" phase of early childhood is of great importance for personal development: it allows the child to acquire images of life that they need, especially for their emotional domain (and it would certainly be wrong for educators to try to influence the child towards prematurely abandoning their imaginary creatures in favor of reality-based achievements, for example through certain early learning methods!). However, it's an important step of maturation when the child's thinking and speech come closer to reality

– this roughly corresponds to school age and vocational maturity. Of course, there's great variability in the timing and manner of adaptation, and of course, the family model of truth also plays a decisive role. Nonetheless, educators must by no means reproach the child for not aligning with "our" reality in their speech, but rather, they must understand and accept it as a necessary stage of the child's development.

## Children's statements and their evaluation

However, it can become dangerous when one adopts a non-critical attitude towards the linguistic expressions of the young child, which unfortunately happens quite often if it's not understood that the child, in their "illusionistic phase," uses the same language as adults but their discourse expresses something entirely different. And it's particularly dangerous when the adult starts asking questions when the child reports an "experience," without considering how their questions might have a suggestive effect on the child, who can be led – generally without any malicious intent initially – to invent entirely absurd stories.

The child immediately realizes they are being taken seriously, feels at the center of a sensation, and lets their imagination flourish. Details are added, partly from the questions, but also from their own "material," some of which might lead some to believe that "such a small child cannot invent such things!" This can lead to tragic consequences when a child suddenly finds themselves at the center of a sexual case: an older man is accused of sexually abusing a little girl. The child draws the necessary "material" (with astonishing details) from expressions they've overheard incidentally – again, not believed is what a child can comprehend in adult conversations; but many things are then "suggested" to the child once the case is underway. Thus, an innocent person can truly find themselves in danger of suffering serious harm within the intricacies of the justice system, unless an expert familiar with these issues puts things into perspective.

Similar to the first part of this chapter where the respect for property was discussed, the child also matures to align their speech with real facts and take responsibility for the truth ("pay homage to the truth," as it's nicely put in a somewhat outdated formulation today). Certainly, this involves a painful renunciation on the part of the child. This is also perceptible in the beginning of a fairy tale by the Grimm brothers: "There was a time when wishes were still granted..."; and this is part of what Sigmund Freud referred to as the "discontent in civilization."

It's indeed rare for a young child to cause problems with their fantasies. In general, parents can rejoice in their child playing with reality. They can trust that this will transform in due time, develop, and eventually result in the child acknowledging reality. Patience can be exercised in this process – as having the ability to wait is a significant skill for an educator. Under no circumstances should feelings of guilt be awakened in the child by launching zealous accusations that they're a liar.


## Childish "Lies"

In this domain as well, there's a developmental childishness of personality that becomes dangerous when advanced thinking and speech faculties are employed for the child's fantasies, such that what's put forth seems very plausible and can truly deceive the environment. This then requires good criticism, a conscientious comparison with objectively verifiable facts, to arrive at an accurate evaluation.

Moralizing, passing moral judgment on all these childish fantasies should be avoided; it would be detrimental to the child. However, it's also normal for a child who's done something against the rules to seek exoneration or even lie while downplaying their wrongdoings. It's a form of necessary protection that a child normally learns quite swiftly. (It goes without saying that an educator shouldn't fall into this trap and should seek to uncover what actually happened!) But once the order of things is restored, the child shouldn't be held too accountable for such behavior; it should be understood that it's necessary for self-assertion in life.


## Other Pathological Behaviors

What distinctly stands out as pathological behavior from this "normal behavior" is when the child – and here we include children with "instinctual disorders" – isn't able to escape with words when cornered, but openly admits to everything they've done, not even attempting to conceal what could incriminate them (they even provide details that others aren't yet aware of).

Educators who aren't themselves confident in their instincts feel compelled to morally evaluate such behavior positively: the child clearly sees how badly they've acted; this "awareness" should also lead to improvement for everyone in the future! Unfortunately, that's not the case in reality. These "pure naifs" constantly continue to make mistakes, perpetually find themselves in distressing situations they can't escape from.

Yet, even at a young age, malicious lies exist, defamation to harm others – whether it's to deflect one's own actions onto others or simply out of sheer spite (in autistic children – see this chapter! – we find such events that attest to the profound nature of these types).

The lies of hysterical personalities have a particular coloration – they must be described in this chapter.

## Educational therapy

This brings us to the therapeutic and educational issue: how should the educator behave towards a child who doesn't tell the truth? Undoubtedly, education used to be too harsh, too repressive, too influenced by the moral conceptions of adults that weren't suited to the child, without understanding that the child's free play with their imagination is a necessary stage of their development.

Certainly, the good father, the good educator, will provide the child with material for their imaginary games and give them stimuli (Nietzsche's saying applies here as well: "In the just person, there lives a child who wants to play!" And how many model trains are bought mainly because it's the father who wants to play!).

But the father shows, more through their attitude than through a preached demand, that they value reality and truth – if they truly do! Adults often don't realize how much they use lies daily to easily escape unpleasant situations, how much they enjoy gossiping about others. So, it's probably ineffective to ask children to meet demands that one doesn't fulfill themselves in their own lives. Education about truth must be conducted with care: by maintaining a critical distance from what's presented, patiently seeking out what was real, and showing that "lies have short legs" and that only truth and reality endure. This thus opens up the space of freedom accessible to humans, the goal of personality development. When one contrasts the biblical saying: "The truth will set you free" with Hegel's statement: "Freedom is the understanding of necessity," one recognizes that both mean the same thing: a lofty objective to be achieved with all reason and heart.

## The Runaway

The runaway, the act of fleeing from home, is also an event motivated by very diverse reasons, carried out by very different characters.

There are those who are impulsive and lack inhibition (often due to a cerebral disorder) who run away from home without a real reason, without a deeper conflict preceding it. Even if they seem attached to their family at certain moments, these conditions are not enough to hold them back. Nothing is planned, nothing is prepared, nothing is taken with them, things that would be necessary for such a project. Everything is done on a sudden decision, but it's executed very skillfully, obstacles are overcome with ease (we've witnessed directly how such a boy escaped from a special education facility: nothing had happened before that could explain the event; suddenly, there was a flash in his eyes – and he was gone! Impossible to stop or catch him).

The abrupt runaway is also a well-known symptom of epileptic twilight states of consciousness. The term "twilight state" is fitting. It's not the clear light of consciousness in which fully responsible actions take place, but rather a "twilight" of varying degrees of dimness; this can lead to events that still appear quite rational – for instance, someone buys a train ticket at the station, indicates a specific destination, gets on a train, but then, once the abnormal state is over, finds themselves disoriented in an unfamiliar area, not knowing how they got there. Only through very attentive observation does one notice that such a person is in an abnormal state of consciousness. In the electroencephalogram (EEG), series of seizure potentials are found during these states, which often last a long time. This form of fugue isn't motivated externally, it doesn't precede any conflict. Only the abnormal brain state triggers something like this.

The diagnosis can be confirmed through the EEG and "ex juvantibus," through the success of anti-epileptic therapy. This form of epileptic "attacks" has its "age-related typing": it only appears at a later school age and in adolescents.

Among these quite abnormal states, there are clearly cases of runaway motivated by the child's situation. A frequent reason is fear, often related to school. One doesn't dare to face the demands: tomorrow, a school assignment looms, or there's already a bad grade in the bag and one doesn't dare go home, or an important task remains uncompleted. In such situations, you can see how fear can grip a child to the extent that no more reflection intervenes to regulate the situation. The child knows very well that what they're doing is very unreasonable - and yet, they do the irrational: this is essential to true anxiety neurosis. Under the suffering and self-reproach, the child flees from home - this home now shines in the child's mind in the most beautiful light, like a lost paradise: how warm it would be, how lovely it would be if everyone were sitting at the table at home! The boy shivers through the night in the ruins of a construction site or at the edge of the forest, scared of every noise, ghostly apparitions appear; but the decision to return home isn't made.

Very different things can happen: hunger and the desire to return home become unbearable – and one eventually returns home as the prodigal son – or the child is intercepted, their agency is taken away, and they are happy about it! Such an event even has the chance to be "cathartic," to set an improvement of the entire situation in motion: the teacher who realizes with horror all that could have happened decides to show more understanding towards the child and parents seek to change, to adapt more; and the child learns what was wrong, how things could be done better. Thus, they can draw real maturation impulses from the frightening event. Those who have lived with a child the feeling of relief, even elevation, a deeper self-awareness after such an event, understand what the term "felix culpa" – the "fortunate fall" – means in Christian philosophy: although sin and guilt should be avoided, it can end so well through grace that a person becomes better, happier (felix) after guilt than they could have been without it.

Lastly, there's also the planned runaway, out of curiosity, thoughtfully considered and prepared, sometimes with one or more companions. This is where the camaraderie of boys who gather to act together, to run away or steal, comes into play. This mostly occurs in adolescence, where dangerous "gangs" form, but also already in children.

The laws according to which such group formations occur are complex. Certainly, the boys have a lot in common. They all come from a deteriorating environment – which certainly doesn't mean they belong to the "lower" social strata of our modern society. They often come from very affluent backgrounds, but the stability and cohesion of the family are always disturbed, there's the disastrous situation of luxury's decline, equally severe as the decline of poverty! But in terms of character qualities, the children and adolescents who gather for antisocial actions are very different – and it's precisely for this reason that they find each other. A less vital, inactive boy without orientation needs a leader who tells them what they should do, which they then follow without will; similarly, the boy with leadership qualities needs other people who follow them, over whom they exert their power. Often, it's not even the leader who carries out the act, but rather the passive ones without their own impulses. And in each individual case, there are other personality qualities that bind individuals to each other, which need to be discovered if one wants to clarify the motives and offer personal help.

However, these experiences clearly show that experiences don't happen randomly to a person and don't shape them; there's a reciprocal relationship between experience and personality. The individual shapes their experiences just as these experiences shape the individual. Both, experience and personality, combine to form a higher unity.

Child runaways are generally the result of a long tragic history. This shows that the child in question has been deprived of many things during their development, especially a rootedness in a family. The only true solution would be for parents to reflect on their task, to take better care of the child, perhaps even to come together again, to give their community meaning once more. However, often this path is no longer feasible, too many things have been destroyed and exhausted in the family situation. Other measures are then attempted, such as placement in an institution.

The advantage of such administration lies in the fact that the child is protected from themselves, given time to mature, and the means of good educational guidance can be utilized. But in recent years, it has become clear that institutional placement can also have considerable disadvantages. In a group that's too large and too homogenous (consisting solely of children of the same age), it's not possible to develop normal interpersonal relationships with a stable reference person; the institution is very isolated from the reality of the world, making integration into it more difficult. This becomes particularly serious when institutional placement has to be changed due to behavioral difficulties, or even several times.

# IX/ CHILDREN AND ANXIETY (1982)

## The biological law of anxiety

Anxiety problems in children delve into the depths of human existence. It's not so simple to analyze and treat fear in all cases. No, fear is part of being human! Terence's words remain valid for all times: "I am a human being, nothing human is foreign to me" – and this essentially includes fear, as Goethe's verse proves: "Shivering is the finest part of humanity." One could propose the idea that fear is linked to all major stages of a child's development according to a biological law. An example would be the "fear of eight months" in very young children, as described by René Spitz (but based on our own observations, it can also occur much earlier, around five months): the child, who was open and friendly towards all human faces during the first months of their life, suddenly reacts with fear and rejection when a stranger's face appears, responding "sthenically" with angry screams and kicks, and then "asthenically" by withdrawing. We are convinced that this fear is causally correlated with a developmental progression: the childlike person gains "contours," a self-awareness emerges – "I am me, and you are outside!" – and this "outside" seems strange and dangerous until the stranger gains the child's trust by waiting patiently and approaching with friendly expressions. In southern regions of Germany, this event is also called "foreigner" (the child "feels foreign") and that aptly describes what happens in the child.

In the further development of the child, similar fears exist that unfold similarly and are caused similarly: alongside the surges of personal maturation, the acquisition of linguistic understanding, and the knowledge of the world. However, this growing awareness of the world isn't only pleasant for the child: they realize the amount of strange and dangerous things in the world, especially since they often experience them in a "magical" way (the magical world of fairy tales is indeed suited to the child in all eras and cultures!).

However, in normal circumstances – meaning when the child has a healthy constitution and is well integrated into their family environment – "what saves grows as well" (Hölderlin): the child experiences that they can overcome dangers, they have trust in the protection of their loved ones and cling to it – and thus, they surpass fear. It's not uncommon to observe that a child goes through several phases of fear during their early childhood and generally emerges from them with enhanced development.

One could assume that this development is significant, that overcome – yet still present – fear is closely linked to the spontaneity and creativity of the human being, that it is a powerful "motif of perfection." Poets, who are the best interpreters of human existence, have impressively described it, as Rilke did in his poem "Childhood": "The fear of school and passing time" and "oh senseless sadness, oh dream, oh horror." The "motivating function" of fear is vividly described in Michelangelo's sonnets, in Hans Pfitzner's "Palestrina" – and most of all in the entire work of Søren Kierkegaard, as well as in the writings of existentialist philosophers, of whom Kierkegaard is the "precursor."

## Constitutional Factors

However, not all children follow the "normal" path – and that's when they need psychotherapeutic help. These are the "healthy primitives," who are well "merged" (integrated) with themselves and the world, who are least tormented by fear and feel secure "at home," who know how to deal well with the world; they don't really notice what's profound and strange in it.

These are the differentiated, more finely organized, more sensitive children who are much more prone to anxiety; it seems their nervous system is too delicate an instrument that easily becomes imbalanced – and that provokes fear! It might be internal processes they observe with excessive self-observation and find distressing, such as heartbeats (is it going to stop now? – and this can actually cause arrhythmias) or micropsy (objects in the external world seem abnormally small) or other bodily processes. Such "intellectualization" or "problem-making" often disrupts autonomous and unconscious processes – Hamburger refers to them as "attention neuroses." These children don't feel "at home" in their own bodies – they're often grotesquely clumsy, they lack a "body schema" – and what happens in their bodies is strange, unfamiliar, and frightening to them.

Events in the external world are often experienced as disturbing by these hyper-differentiated children: natural phenomena, storms (and they also know very early that this can actually be dangerous and insist on having lightning rods where they live), but especially darkness and the faint auditory and visual impressions that are so different in the dark (like furniture creaking or light passing through a window); animals, dogs, and insects also become strange, and the dangers they present are superstitiously overestimated; finally, incomprehensible technical processes like the sound of toilets.

## External factors

We previously explained that children can be predisposed to anxiety and be affected by it more due to their innate psychological characteristics. Now, it's necessary to discuss the causes that reside in the environment, especially in the educational context. It's not entirely true – or at least not completely true – that external events are always the cause of anxiety in children, as parents generally believe, especially mothers, even though impressive events are often reported.

Rather, the question arises: do experiences only come "from the outside" to human beings, simply sent by chance? Or isn't there an internal disposition to undergo certain experiences, determined, at least in part, by pre-existing psychological characteristics? Regarding the issue of anxiety, isn't it true that pre-existing anxiety literally attracts certain experiences? A typical example: is it the fault of the dog if the child experiences prolonged anxiety after being barked at or bitten by it?

But isn't it more true that it's through the child's anxious behavior that they provoked the dog's reaction? The normal child approaches the animal freely and confidently – and the dog responds with confidence, friendliness, unless it's a psychopathic dog! And vice versa: the self-assured child goes through dangers, often without even noticing them – this is beautifully described in the tale "The Boy Who Set Out to Learn What Fear Was." We've tried to describe the endogenous roots of anxious behavior (it should be noted that in many cases, a hereditary transmission, usually from the mother's side, is evident). Now, it's necessary to discuss the causes related to the environment, to education.

The greatest importance undoubtedly lies in the absence or loss of affective relationships, particularly in early childhood. We described at the beginning of this chapter the interplay between recognizing danger and strangeness in the world – and establishing the equilibrium, the trust that is constantly restored when the child finds the fertile ground for their rooting in the world. It's dreadful for a child not to have the conditions of mental health due to an accident or human failure.

Bowlby and René Spitz have poignantly described these conditions as a "deprivation syndrome" – the profound insecurity, fear, uprooting, disruption of interpersonal relationships that mark these individuals throughout their lives.

## Children of Divorce

The fate of children from divorced families is an ocean of suffering that spreads in our era, where the old values are largely in ruins. Very early on, well before the official divorce and separation of parents, battles break out, destroying the ground on which the child could have rooted themselves in the world, as we described. Unresolved sexual tensions, which become apparent to the child even if attempts are made to hide them, are a source of their anxiety (as opposed to effective sex education through experiencing parental love!).

Once the parents' separation has taken place, the struggles

usually continue, with the former partners rarely overcoming their disappointment. And even if they strive not to involve the child, the child perceives the glances and "half-spoken words" of one of the parents, which convey the situation between the two. And they are inevitably drawn into the conflict. There is a battle for the child's affection, they're bought with gifts and promises. But how can a young child find their own position in such a situation? A great insecurity is inevitable. And all too often, one of the parents, usually the one with whom the child lives, uses the child as a ruthless weapon in a fight against the other parent, filling them with hatred towards that parent (and hatred is a "killer of humanity"!). A. Portmann speaks in this context of a "social inheritance": there's not only a "genetic" inheritance (transmitted through chromosomes), but there's also a transmission of central social behavior to descendants, "like an inheritance" – and then a life's destiny follows the course of the lived situation. In line with this social inheritance, the child of divorce is severely disturbed in their interpersonal relationships, tormented by anxiety throughout their life and, in the long term, unable to lead a fulfilled marital life. Thus, those who have experienced these problems note that the parents, even the grandparents of children from divorced families, also come from broken marriages. And no matter how well-founded a court decision is, no matter how well-advised medical or psychotherapeutic counseling may be, it can't truly help such children; their misery is incurable!

## Overprotection

The situation described above is an extreme example of the

lack of appropriate emotional attention towards a child, resulting from hateful conflicts between parents, which can only lead to severe insecurity and anxiety for the child. However, the opposite excess can also have similar consequences: too much attention, excessive care (the famous "overprotection"). Often, due to the mother's anxiety, in order to avoid potential dangers for the child, every opportunity for them to prove themselves, to become autonomous, is taken away. Thus, the interplay between exploring the unknown (even if it might be frightening) and testing oneself, exercising one's own strengths with all the associated "functional joy," is disrupted, even though it is the most effective way to combat innate fear.

And in the same way that children who suffer from a "deprivation" of love have an increased predisposition to anxiety, those who are treated with excessive "overprotection" are also more prone to anxiety; they enter life weakened, unable to cope. In both cases, a recognition of the child's independence is lacking.

In the dilemma of finding the right balance between these two opposites, the key is likely this: to respect the child as a person, not belonging to anyone in particular – which is compatible with guidance and accompaniment, exercised with proper authority.

Now let's return to what was addressed at the beginning of this chapter. The phases of a child's maturation are always periods of particular predisposition to anxiety. We explained this for the "fear of strangers" in the early months of life, where a first "self-awareness" of the individual is accompanied by specific anxiety, and these two phenomena are visibly closely linked.

Very similar things happen in the later stages of a child's

development. The child's exploration of the world, the rapid acquisition of knowledge conveyed through language, the establishment of relationships between things, which also opens up an insight into the unknown and the unsettling – all of this brings about a new specific anxiety, especially in children predisposed to endogenous anxiety (who are precisely the most differentiated, the most sensitive).

Later, as the child becomes a toddler or enters early school age, they enter broader communities, such as kindergarten and school. Ties with the family loosen, the mother and father are no longer the sole reference figures (and even that can already be a source of insecurity for the child). A new and vast realm opens up to them: social learning becomes paramount, the "group dynamics" with all the differentiated and complex relationships come into play.

And this has implications that can often be traumatic, especially when the child has challenges to overcome: motor clumsiness or even cerebral palsy that prevents them from asserting themselves in "position battles," or a disorder in regulating instincts that prevents them from finding the right words, the right action at the right time, but makes them appear ridiculous, at any rate inferior. This can plunge the child into great anxiety, up to the refusal to go to school and fleeing.

During the school years, it's not just about acquiring knowledge, but also about awakening the desire for achievement, mental activity is elevated to a higher level, guided and controlled by the realities of life. Personal interests begin to develop, the future professional choice sometimes already seems to be taking shape. In the majority of cases, this development is experienced happily by the child, and this phase generally represents a period of joyful and confident maturation for the child.

However, in some particular cases, there are internal and external threats. Performance expectations and thinking and working capacities are not in balance. It's possible that the increasing demands for abstract and logical thinking cannot be met, or there might be a lack of concentration (the "focus" on the task at hand). Time passes without results, participation in class and assignments are not successful. Similarly, disruption can be caused from the outside. The teacher's teaching method might not be engaging enough to captivate even those initially inattentive. They might also talk over the child's head, underestimating their capabilities, thus overwhelming them with a sense of defeat and reinforcing it through punitive methods, creating a lasting burden. The home learning environment is often insufficient, even traumatic.

The working mother doesn't have time to accompany learning properly, and the most often chosen recourse, sending the child to a learning center or boarding school, brings no success: the child, who would need individual guidance in the individual situation, doesn't benefit from group lessons. But even when the mother makes herself available to help the child learn, it often doesn't go well: precisely because she is so emotionally attached to the child, she can't bear to see her darling performing poorly; she becomes irritable, scolds, and even strikes (and this certainly doesn't serve the child).

Failure to meet performance demands can be a source of severe anxiety for the child. This has always been the case. An example is the touching story by Marie von Ebner-Eschenbach, titled "The Favorite," where a sensitive but less robust boy succumbs to suicide because he fails to meet his own and others' performance expectations (this was around the turn of the century when rapid industrialization led to significant social transformations and consequent tensions). It's possible that the pressure of performance at school, fueled also by parents, is even stronger today than in the past – in any case, this is generally lamented and fought against by young people. The old values that used to integrate parents and children into a way of life and created conditions conducive to harmonious personality development have disappeared or are disappearing. Ruthless competition reigns, and children must be prepared to face it; where there are limitations on available spots (numerus clausus), this competition can often be destructive. Many young people vehemently fight against these attitudes, condemn the economic and social conditions that lead to such situations, and in response to this uncertainty and fear, engage in behaviors that, in turn, often lead to the destruction of their personalities (we think of addictive behaviors, a serious social danger of our time!).

## Puberty and the Anxiety Issue

Now we enter the realm of the period that follows compulsory schooling, namely puberty and adolescence. It's understandable that there are ample reasons to be anxious during this time, given how this phase of development is filled with contradictions and disharmonies. Certainly, puberty is the stage of highest intellectual development, of the ability for abstraction and introspection. The experience of new internal developments brings about a feeling of exhilaration, a new sense of strength. But this self-assuredness isn't without opposition:

when confronted with reality, the inadequacy of one's own performance often becomes apparent; the feeling of exhilaration can abruptly turn into a depressive feeling, even despair and disgust for life. The experience of sexuality, which now asserts itself with strong dynamism, is also marked by contrasts: new and formidable possibilities for self-fulfillment, the possibility of finding the ultimate fulfillment of human existence in another beloved being, but also the danger of taking sexuality too seriously, of feeling self-disgust, cynicism, and defeatism towards life, the possibility of feeling guilty in front of others. This has always been a source of tragedy, which cannot be overcome with the yet untested powers of personality in this phase; however, this is particularly dangerous in our time, where the sexualized atmosphere, the "common sense," only releases inhibitions and devalues anything that could provide anchoring and orientation for a young person. All these fundamental changes, the lifting of taboos on modesty and sexuality, fail to eliminate anxiety, which is fundamentally linked to the sexual domain, even in young people particularly predisposed to anxiety (this is not only due to "repressions" that could be resolved through psychoanalytic analysis). Precisely in this area, the "ambivalence" of all emotions is manifest (as Sigmund Freud so brilliantly described). However, the negative aspect of this contradictory emotional attitude is primarily anxiety, which is considered by existentialist philosophers of our time as the "fundamental state of human existence."

But just as in the younger stages, where the specific insecurities and anxieties of each phase are generally overcome to lead to renewed confidence and an important stage of development, the same applies to the phase we have just described: from here, the path of life continues on the paths already taken (the great coming-of-age novels from various literatures testify to this). We should learn from all of this how much anxiety naturally plays a part in the grand journey of human self-discovery, of the separation of the child from the maternal soil from which they originated, which was certainly necessary for the initial processes of maturation, but must ultimately be abandoned so that the individual can "become themselves," and this journey is marked by anxiety as an important factor that accompanies – and certainly stimulates – the stages of maturation.

What matters above all is what each individual "does with their anxiety," whether they develop psychic strengths to make them fertile in constructing their personality or whether they suffer from them helplessly and are thus hindered in their maturation.

## Psychosomatic manifestations

Let's now discuss the disabilities and illness symptoms caused by anxiety. This is where the vast domain of psychosomatic symptomatology opens up. For some of these clinical pictures, the close link with anxiety is evident to specialists. First, let's mention enuresis and encopresis, both daytime and nighttime. If a child who was already potty-trained regresses to these behaviors that are very stressful for those around them, in some cases, it's likely that they might not dare to cross the required step of maturation towards independence due to fear: they "want" to remain or become infantile again, so they would need care corresponding to that given to a young child. Sometimes, a careful examination might also reveal a traumatic event that could have triggered such a "regression."

Another symptom that clearly shows a link with anxiety is "morning vomiting" or "school vomiting." A child feels inadequate in the face of school demands, rightly or underestimating their own abilities and the real demands that appear insurmountable to them; sometimes, it's indeed a too strict teacher who scares the child. One could describe morning vomiting, which so clearly indicates the anxious rejection of an overwhelming situation, as the "language of the organ," but one could also argue that vegetative connections are used that are intended during the transition from the "trophotropic" sleep phase to the "ergotropic" wake phase of the organism (even normally, there are difficulties felt as very unpleasant by sensitive individuals). In any case, the "gain from illness" in this symptomatology is considerable: a child who is "so ill" that they vomit, of course, "cannot" go to school – and thus escapes the anxiety-inducing situation (these pressures, as well as the accompanying vegetative symptoms, are masterfully described in the story of Hanno Buddenbrook by Thomas Mann). However, this gain is only apparent: the situation isn't resolved, the solution is only postponed, or even complicated in reality. If we truly want to help the child, we need to remove them from this difficult situation, which will be described shortly. It's worth noting only that anxiety-related symptoms can also manifest in many other organs. Clarification of the genesis is an important prerequisite for successful therapy (of course, this doesn't apply without exception: sometimes, psychosomatic symptoms can be managed without identifying the underlying causes; see our "suggestive therapy" section!).

<u>**Therapy**</u>

At the end of this chapter, it's necessary to discuss what repeatedly appears as the goal of the entire work: the therapeutic issue of anxiety. If the reader accepts what was said at the beginning of the section, that anxiety is universally human, then psychotherapy should only concern particularly troublesome forms of anxiety, those that endanger the personality.

First, let's examine what intellectual clarification of the causes of anxiety can achieve. By informing the child about the realities, the natural and physical causes of events, anxiety can lose much of its frightening character. The child can learn to manage things better; they no longer seem strange but rather familiar. However, it must be understood that rational explanations have a very limited effect on the child's experience, not only because doubts arise in them about whether "this applies specifically to this thing" (Goethe). The main reason for the ineffectiveness of intellectual explanation, however, lies in the following fact: existentialist philosophy, expressing a human truth, distinguishes between fear related to reality and anxiety that often arises without real foundation, coming from the depths of the emotional realm of the person and tormenting precisely because it cannot be rationally justified. Thus, clarification doesn't always cure anxiety, and it's highly doubtful that this can always be achieved through complex psychoanalytic methods, whether interpreting the child's play or using other classical analytical methods; continuous self-critical questioning would be necessary to know whether something is not being "projected" onto the child, something that is not actually active within them (in this context, it's worthwhile to read what Anna Freud – "the great daughter of an immortal man," E. Jones – critically writes about child analysis: according to her, it's only useful in rather rare cases).

One thing is certain, however: those who must deal with anxious children – be they parents, educators, or psychotherapists – must be capable of mastering their own anxiety through the use of adult reasoning and mature responsibility; what counts here is the emotional attitude, not what the mother says to her child. If she is afraid herself, despite her reassuring words, the child notices it very well, and this leads to the dreaded "duo" of anxiety, in which the mother and the child "play" their own role, as the child generally becomes scared when feeling the mother's anxiety, and in turn, the mother is dismayed by the child's anxiety symptoms (the same applies to the relationship between animals and humans: the animal unfailingly senses if the human is afraid of it, of its superior bodily strength; only the fearless trainer can succeed).

## Educational-therapeutic management

In the "pedagogical-therapeutic direction" of the anxious child, it is important to provide them with the opportunity to engage in an activity that brings them success. Artistic creation is the most beneficial; the child can symbolically represent their anxiety through it, which in itself is a liberating act. We know that artists have always done the same thing everywhere: liberate themselves from their anxiety, which is often particularly strong in very sensitive individuals, through their work. This is one of the most difficult yet also most useful tasks of the educator – to encourage the child in such activities, to assist them with technical problems, but without forcing them, without pushing them in certain stylistic directions (which unfortunately happens all too often in the art education of our schools and hampers children's creativity).

However, even more important than practicing a specific technique is the pedagogical-therapeutic support provided to the child through their human involvement. The therapist stands alongside the child, which in Latin means "inter-esse," "to be there" – with their own courage, their audacity. This is just as "contagious" as the mother's fear (which so discourages the child). The fearless attitude of the educator convinces much more than many fervent arguments: life is not without hope, one can succeed in facing the world.

In many cases, however, the child is so entangled in their mother's anxiety (no matter where this attitude of the mother might stem from) that it's impossible to separate them. Therefore, it's often necessary to remove the child from their family for a certain period and admit them to a pedagogical or psychiatric therapy unit for children. This is where group dynamics, the team comes into play: doctor, psychologist, teacher, and educator – none of them fear with the child; equally effective is coexistence with peers engaging in joyful activities throughout the day. They all involve the anxious child in communal life, and anxiety gradually crumbles away, so to speak, layer by layer – it no longer "possesses" the child, and it even becomes laughable for them, especially since they often possess heightened self-reflection!

## Self-Knowledge

A final step must be described as cautiously as necessary. We have already mentioned that anxious children are often psychologically highly differentiated, very sensitive. Their own deep experience shows them how strange and dangerous the world is. Sometimes, it is truly helpful to guide such a child towards the realization that anxiety has a purpose in their life, that it is a "catalyst towards perfection." However, this cannot be suggested to them, as that could lead to a neurotic approach and only intensify anxiety. Instead, the therapist must provoke the child's awareness through empathetic questions, allowing them to arrive at the conclusion of accepting themselves as they have been shaped and molded by fate. This goal, as we have learned, is not too high. Differentiated children are sometimes capable of achieving such levels of understanding as early as primary school. The thought developed here is similar to what Viktor Frankl undertakes in his "logotherapy": aiding the suffering human in their "search for meaning," through clarifying speech, to discover the meaning of their life.

In this part of our work, the entire diversity of human possibilities and human suffering is reflected, along with the hope of being able to provide assistance through humanity. The struggle on the "battlefield of life" is not without hope.

# X/ EXCESS AND DEPENDENCE (1981)

An unforgettable experience: we are in Delphi - and immediately, it becomes clear to us that this has been a sacred place since time immemorial. The sea is far away, from where most of the pilgrims came. And behind us rises the steep cliff of Mount Parnassus, torn by ravines, flown over by eagles. The spring of Castalia, which once quenched and inspired poets, has dried up - but the place is still magnificent. And our guide, still captivated by the ancient grandeur, tells the story: how Phoebus Apollo descended from Parnassus after slaying the Python dragon in a fierce battle, the dragon personifying dark and primal forces; but Apollo, the resplendent victor, represents the new era: that of intellectual clarity, mastery over impulses, understanding of nature where, though always threatened, the True, the Good, and the Beautiful must reign. At the foot of the steep cliff, where the fall finds a moment of rest, where the spring also gushes forth, a sanctuary has stood since unfathomable times. Apollo commands the priests residing there to build him a temple, an eternal memorial to his victory. On both sides of the pediment, according to his instructions, it is said, inscriptions will be placed - on the front: "Xrwit," "gnothi sauton," "know thyself!" on the rear: "iMitv afar," "meden agan," "nothing in excess, exercise moderation!" And these two words, I believe, embody the West, which has traversed a long and painful history, to which we still hold fast. He who knows himself, who confronts himself critically and responsibly, will also do what is just; and he who exercises moderation, who does not exceed the limits, lives in peace with himself and with the community. All of this is contained within these concise words. And it continues throughout our shared history.

The essence of all this is determined by Roman "virtus," measured masculine virtue, which is useful and fit for life, soon elevated in the heights of a life shaped by religion in the work of Saint Benedict, celebrated this year here in Salzburg. And "diu maze," practicing moderation, was a central demand of the chivalrous Middle Ages. The great epics of that time, written as examples of shaped life and with evident educational intent, illustrate the importance of this principle in particular.

It is appropriate to counter an error from the outset that can creep into such discussions. "Measure" does not mean mediocrity, the "aurea mediocritas," in which one lives comfortably because they have relinquished the tensions of life. Especially young people, as well as "progressive" educators who guide them, think that this carries a connotation of senility. This basic attitude is attributed to the elderly: "they have everything behind them / and are, thank God, virtuous" - but the one who said that was Wilhelm Busch, a solitary, malicious, incapable of love, depressive man, who saw the world through his dark, skeptical (which certainly had grandeur!) and despairing lenses.

As responsible educators, we must also address what the demand for moderation means for today's youth. The thesis that will emerge from these developments is as follows: humans are always in danger of losing measure, it is deeply ingrained in their existence (otherwise the warning would not be carved on the temple at Delphi); young people are particularly exposed to this danger, and today, it manifests in the most pronounced manner.

Man, liberated - or expelled - from the security offered by instinctual regulations, seeks with his intellect means and methods to confront the dangers of the world. He gains power over nature - but he mistreats it just as much (we did not realize, at a time when our power was not as great, the dangers to which we expose ourselves). The ambition to dominate nature with our arts (that is, the Greek word "techne," which gave birth to technology) has never taken proper measure into account; it always ruthlessly aimed toward the future (when the wise Greek said he would lift the Earth off its hinges, it would only require giving him a point to place the lever - that certainly doesn't sound moderate).

It is only late in history that men, or at least a few voices in the desert, become aware of the danger of losing measure; we must backtrack, or else we will destroy nature, ravage the beautiful blue planet, Earth.

The dangers of losing measure are greatest during adolescence. The processes in which new things form within the young, both on a physical level (especially endocrine) and mental (fundamental restructuring of self-consciousness) - have an element of intoxication and are also experienced as such by the young: "youth is intoxication without wine," they have always said. Measure is neither sought nor found in those moments. Educators should understand that a certain moderation can be requested in the face of the extremes that play out in young people during puberty. Preaching moderation in this regard would only accentuate the generational divide - such requests already provoke the white-haired youth. But this "biological" misunderstanding, so to speak, deeply wounds both sides. This leads to premature condemnations that bring neither understanding nor improvement, but only reinforce bitterness.

Another fact must be discussed before we address our main subject: contemporary forms of excess and addiction. If we cast a glance at the history of humanity and at countries around the world, we always observe this passionate aspiration to transcend oneself in ecstasy, to surpass oneself, even to expand human consciousness (Aldous Huxley exerted a dangerously seductive influence on the youth of his time with his book bearing this title). We will later address the devastating effects of drugs on personality. However, it is certain that intoxication can awaken creative impulses in individuals gifted with genius - and here lies the importance! - and that some geniuses can only create in a state of intoxication (much like an emerging illness, such as cerebral megalomania, has unleashed their creativity, driving them to action - Nietzsche and Maupassant are troubling examples). Nonetheless, intoxication does not lead to genius itself; it only reveals the personality that plunges into it. It must be emphasized, though, that intoxication, the alteration of brain reactivity caused by certain drugs, truly exerts a mysterious fascination over the human being. The Greeks, among the wisest of all peoples, associated Dionysus with Apollo, Phoebus: Apollo embodies clarity, even moderated thought that avoids hybris, the sacrilege of excessive passion, while Dionysus is the god of intoxication. What were they seeking in him? "This enrichment that life can experience, this fact of being carried by the life stream, the pleasure of possibilities that do not demand to be seized in excess and infinity" (v. Gebsattel). The individual seeks to preserve their psychic balance in reaction to a drought of existence, to an obstruction of principles. And they seek euphoria, the feeling that makes everything difficult and oppressive feel lighter (of course, this systematically comes with the following effects: hangovers, depression, which will be discussed later). Up until now, we have examined the general criteria of humanity and the typical characteristics of different phases of development. Now, in the main part of our presentation, it is essential to discuss manifestations of addiction in the present and in our culture. It is clear to all responsible parties that alarming changes have occurred in this regard. The opulent situation of Western countries offers a multitude of substances capable of altering consciousness, including drugs from the East, the Middle East, and the Far East. This has become an enormous market. The complete absorption of addicts toward the addictive substance bestows immense power upon the distributor: not only the power of money but also the power to take complete control over others (which certainly constitutes a strong motivation for the "dealer"). However, modern times have also introduced onto the market a massive supply of pharmaceutical products that can lead to addiction: hypnotics, analgesics, and sedatives (intended to alleviate or eliminate unbearable tensions, promote sleep and oblivion, reduce the state of consciousness as a whole - but of course, tensions are not truly resolved, the overall situation is only worsened!); and it happens that individuals consume drugs with diametrically opposed effects, sometimes the very same individuals who also take sedative drugs - stimulants intended to increase impulses and elevate the state of consciousness (as if this induces genuine activity capable of solving assigned tasks!). And lastly, what is particularly sought after are substances with psychedelic and hallucinogenic effects that induce a comprehensive alteration of the state of consciousness, causing vivid (literally colorful) dreams and sexual hallucinations (although in these cases, it is certain that the modified personality contributes its own share - which, when described convincingly, exerts a dangerous seductive effect on others). Now, we arrive at the crucial point of our presentation: what primarily drives the youth to abandon all human restraint to this extent and plunge into addiction as into an abyss - for many are perfectly aware of it, even seem to seek it: like an extended suicide, like a self-destruction accepted at least in part. We are accustomed to discussing innate and hereditary factors first in these matters.

Even though modern research often obsessively focuses on environmental and familial conditions, ignoring other aspects, unbiased studies show that there is a significant hereditary predisposition in a high percentage of cases (alcoholism, depression, high suicide rates in the ancestry). However, careful observation has long revealed that there are serious flaws in the family situation of these at-risk youths. The history of these individuals who have become difficult, even impossible, to "socialize" shows what a healthy family can provide in terms of essential imprinting, and how a child can hardly develop healthily in the absence of these factors.

When examining the family structure of youth struggling with addiction, a large number of disturbed or broken families are found, whether due to the father's death or, even worse, through divorce (one figure: among the youths studied by Rosenberg in Australia, only half of those surveyed lived with both parents until the age of 15). But even in the absence of such an overt family breakdown, serious educational mistakes can be identified in many cases - an overly strict, even abusive upbringing, or an overly "protective" upbringing: since adhering to the principle of the right measure lies at the heart of this discussion and the entire symposium, it's easy to understand that a young person cannot attain independence and responsibility if their freedom is restricted, if they are not first "let loose" and then left entirely to their own decisions, so that they can find their own measure (of course, it should be emphasized that, in accordance with biological law, a young child needs intensive guidance until they can truly be "free"). However, the educational mistakes in the families from which dependent individuals originate are not necessarily obvious or clearly recognizable upon thorough analysis. There are cases where the environment appears quite orderly, where negative attitudes and conflicting situations are not discernible to the observer, or they are so ubiquitous that a fully capable person could emerge from the same situation. This teaches us that cause-and-effect relationships in the realm of human beings are not as simple: what hinders a young person's development? What favors it, so that the difficulties they face precisely offer them the opportunity to develop strengths, so that they can thank all their worries - such emergency situations play a significant role in the life stories of important individuals. However limited the space for freedom may be in many cases, rarely exceeded in fleeting moments - it does exist! Man is not entirely manipulable by their situation; they remain "the unknown" ("the unknown man"), ultimately elusive to psychology. But what does the character profile of "the" dependent look like? It is clear that in each individual case, the unique characteristics must be identified - it is only in this way that one can help a person in danger, for they are unique and irreplaceable. However, there are also many common characteristics in characters, recognized by all those who have experience with dependent individuals.

Primarily, a reduced "frustration tolerance" is described: these young people are not capable of enduring failure, pain, intense emotions (grief, abandonment, non-acceptance, confrontation with individuals stronger, more beautiful, more talented) and integrating them properly into their own conception of life - which precisely constitutes a central factor in the philosophy of psychodynamic education. Living with one's emotions, using them for companionship - while being "above" criticism and responsibility, that is, not being "overwhelmed" or dominated by them - must be learned by each person from a young age, knowing that the "oppositional phase" and especially adolescence are critical phases of development, that is, decisive phases (this also includes recognizing that feelings and emotions are not only conditioned by external experience, but also by internal state, and therefore one cannot simply "let go" in this area). If someone has not learned this - either because they lacked the appropriate capacity from within, or because it was not taught by their educators - it's a serious personality flaw. And the possibility of deviating onto the wrong paths, namely that of addiction, is dangerously close. One seeks to avoid pain (especially in those who have a "dystonic" predisposition of the autonomic nervous system), one seeks to euphorize oneself to escape feelings of discomfort, depression - or, with one of the hallucinogens, to escape into a dream world that seems to offer what reality does not. An alteration of relationships with reality (which we have already discussed) also occurs because the "fault" of inappropriate behavior is externalized - and the current general situation in civilized countries seems to favor this. We must return to the concept of the "inner state": feelings, when satisfied or even saturated, easily turn back (which is why nothing is harder to endure than a series of beautiful days where everything is too easy). The modern luxurious situation in which we all live, especially the social class from which a large number of dependent youth come, does not provide satisfaction, but disgust (which can only be expressed in the prevailing vulgar jargon). A "subculture" forms, authentic in its way of dressing, styling hair, speaking, behaving sexually, giving up hygiene, or even hating it. Thus, a path is taken, from which there is often no possible return - because the detrimental effects of addictive drugs then come into play, which we must still discuss. Another risk group for addiction is comprised of unemployed youth who seek, in the delirium induced by drugs, a short-term solution to their desperate situation. But here too, causality is complex: many of these youth exhibit precisely the personality characteristics described above: they have not been able to pursue the difficult path of school or vocational training and have dropped out. However, the tragically serious aspect of our issue has not yet been addressed in the previous developments: it lies in the fact that addiction is a serious illness (the term "addiction" comes from the term "siech," certainly not from "search"!), a disease for which there is no salvation through the dependent individual's efforts alone - the English expression "drug addiction" expresses it well: "Verfallenheit" (decay) indeed! The ruthless enslavement by certain drugs has serious physical and psychological consequences - especially with opioids, notably heroin, but also to a lesser extent with other drugs. Habituation, especially to heroin (the most commonly used hard drug), leads to tolerating and requiring ever-increasing doses ("increased tolerance"). If these doses are not available, or if the drug is suddenly deprived of the addict, it leads to "withdrawal symptoms" that are subjectively extremely painful, but if the organism is already very weakened, can be fatal: severe vegetative symptoms such as sweating, violent vomiting, pain, cramps, delirium, anxiety, or even hallucinatory states, leading to vegetative collapse. The term "abandonment" particularly applies to the psychological behavior of the addict: the will to heal is completely extinguished, mental strength is focused solely on obtaining "the substance," even through serious criminal acts, with complete abandonment of a "bourgeois" existence. What appears as a rejection of a considered normal existence, or even a rejection of human community, an inability to live with it, manifests itself glaringly, certainly already anchored in the "addictive character," it's one of the prerequisites, just like the previously described frustration intolerance; and as in this case, the inability to live in community is reinforced by the destructive processes that follow drug consumption. What happens in the intoxication of opioids, even more so with hallucinogens, but even with cannabis, happens in complete solitude - and even if intoxicating drugs are consumed together, at heroin or cannabis parties, it's only a "shared solitude"!

The cause of such "inhuman" behavior is certainly a profound disturbance of emotions and mindset: P. Schröder defined the "mindset" as the ability to be with others - and that's accurate: it's that aspect of personality through which one perceives what the other emits

158

and radiates towards oneself, and which enables one to engage with them, even to attach with love and loyalty. And it's certainly the suffering of not possessing such capacities that can motivate a person to seek, in intoxication, what is denied to them due to their relational incapacity.

After describing this, it's easy to understand how terribly difficult the treatment of young addicts can be: how to still build humanity in the patient, despite the "endogenous" obstacles - this is the task we need to discuss in conclusion.

However, we would be incomplete if we did not briefly address alcoholism. This is justified by the numerical proportions. There are about 60,000 heroin addicts in West Germany and a tenth of that number in Austria; however, it's known that the actual number could be much higher. The number of alcoholics and even those in danger due to alcohol is much higher though. But during adolescence - and that's primarily what we're interested in here - severe forms of alcoholism that lead to personality destruction are less common; most of the time, menacing consequences (psychosis and fatal liver cirrhosis) only manifest much later.

However, in certain circles of young people, a concerning development has occurred: alcohol is consumed alongside other drugs, especially tranquilizers. However, this quickly leads to a genuine dependence that one becomes hooked on and can hardly escape from. And for a number of these youth, it's the entry into "hard drugs" with all the terrible consequences.

Drinkers belong to very different types - that's what differentiates the issue from what has been described so far. For many, alcohol is literally a means of socializing: they think it can release inhibitions that separate people from each other - this is sung in countless songs, often in kitschy orgies; and as easily as the relaxed atmosphere can turn into irritability, aggression - or sadness! Of course, the individual's personality also comes into play.

The tragic life of Josef Weinheber, whose alcoholism undoubtedly contributed to his unhappy demise, unfolds differently. He suffered from "shame and fear of death" in his struggle against the "understanding poison" (as he already says in an early poem), despair grew, it's truly impossible to appease it in intoxication. But in moments of elevation, he reaches verses like: "distant spring / your most intimate stanza is called measure and silence" (in a poem - in a Sapphic stanza! - about a visit to the tavern). Thus, what Mörike writes about Mozart certainly applies to him too: "Yet, we know that these pains have flowed away, clarified and pure, into that deep source, which, gushing from a hundred golden pipes, inexhaustibly, in the rhythm of its melodies, spreads all the suffering and all the bliss of the human heart." However, in most cases, it's bare misery that manifests when someone falls victim to alcohol: the destruction of deeper human relationships, economic downfall, mental degradation, and physical deterioration.

In a discussion about "excess and dependency" among the youth, a very sinister form of downfall must also be addressed: involvement in one of the "new youth religions," which bears a fatal similarity to addiction, also in terms of unfavorable prognosis.

Young people rally around a leader and savior who either comes from the Far East or uses linguistic and ideological formulas originating from there. (This is also reflected in the fantastical names of the sects: Hare Krishna, Unification Church (Mun), Scientologists, Divine Mission of Salvation, Children of God). Their followers not only abandon all their possessions but also their thoughts and will to this savior; they turn away from society, especially from their own homes, with a sinister hatred; through very effective techniques (sleep deprivation, fasting, guided meditations (the "Transcendental Meditation" is one such slogan), strict abandoned rituals), this leads to a high-level "depersonalization," which is alarmingly similar to what we know about personality destruction through drugs. The leaders have such a strong hold on those they have enslaved that shocking events can occur, like the mass suicide of nearly a thousand young people in Guyana.

How is this possible?, one who cares about human beings asks with concern. Now, religious sentiment and aspiration are unrootable since this species has lived on Earth; but from the very beginning, this aspiration can also be perverted, "unthinkable human sacrifices are made." But we also recognize how difficult it must be to steer young people away from these erroneous paths or at least try to bring them back to measure and humanity. But of course, what are we doing to prevent this from happening? Can these young people remain rooted in the domain of the Church?

This brings us to therapeutic problems. It's easy to understand how difficult this must be, given the understanding of the deep-rootedness of abnormal behaviors in the personality of these young people - and the severity of the damages caused by drugs in many cases. Thus, in certain therapeutic models, failure rates of up to one hundred percent are reported: whether it's where one thinks persuasive and outpatient methods are enough, or in attempts at placement in clinical services that are not entirely dedicated to this therapeutic task in terms of staff and material resources. Success should also not be expected through "criminalizing" addicts, especially the young ones, even if there's agreement to toughen penalties against sellers and distributors (dealers) - but they are too well organized, and only a very small part of them gets caught.

There is consensus that only long-term inpatient treatments offer prospects of success for addicts. It's not only - and not primarily - about medical measures (like managing withdrawal symptoms) but about human interaction. It's about rebuilding humanity, solidarity with others, which have been buried or not yet developed due to chronic intoxication, and providing "developmental assistance" in this area. It's not a question of technique or a specific pedagogical system, but of the therapist's capacity to communicate with the other, to be there for them, to be supportive (for many, it's the first time in their life - and do they truly deserve it? - but does anyone deserve God's grace and human kindness? Isn't it always a gift, given freely, gratia, donum gratis datum?). Such action is part of primitive human encounters.

This requires time and patience. Demanding the impossible from a patient too quickly would bring them back to a desperate state, regressing. The therapy's goal is to allow the patient to find themselves, to guide them to the reality of their life situation; it's also guiding them towards the world of work, an entirely new experience for many, never experienced before. For that, both the patient and the people treating them must accurately recognize their capacities, in order to provide them with successes, which is an important remedy.

To achieve such goals, a well-coordinated team is necessary, certainly under firm leadership but without claiming dominance over other members, with varying levels of education and different methods, but converging towards a common objective, particularly in human solidarity, so that the patient cannot escape this united front of the assisting community. (It is reported that a model institution in Berlin called "Synanon" - "People learn to live" is written on the entrance door - which adopts the communal living form, strictly but encouragingly directed by people already deeply immersed in addiction, and successes are reported that far exceed those of official institutions. But this is probably attributed to the small group and the special drive of the leaders). Healing cannot be spoken of for individuals so severely affected until they have become new people, with effective self-criticism and the ability to be "with others," to assume the responsibilities that arise from it.

The circle of my observations is closing. It's possible, dear listeners, that among you, who hear me speak each year in this place about central educational questions, astonishment or even discomfort has spread today in an increasing manner: why is he talking about such a specialized and extreme subject today? Does this concern us?
Well, you can believe from my years of experience: we draw our understanding of the conditions in which human behavior, especially social behavior, lies primarily from the understanding of extreme variations, serious mental disorders, criminals, addicts. It's from the experience of the opposite that we understand the essential determinants of behavior.

However, this leads us to conclusions that are far more

important - and promising - than the therapeutic tasks of addicts we have just described, namely the problem of how to prevent young people from falling into drug addiction and even pseudo-religious dependence, thus destroying their lives. What are the conditions for healthy development?

Young people need us, their parents, and educators: the bread of love (much more than the bread of food), the bread of time granted to them (despite the demands of work placed on parents - but what a disastrous situation for children left to themselves!); they need our understanding for their typical needs of phase and time (how difficult it is for us, the elderly, who come from a different era!); they need us, the elderly, who have learned to "complete our circle of becoming through renunciation and fulfillment" (Hans Dibold), the example of moderation - as they cannot yet find this moderation themselves, tied to their own law of development.

Throughout the centuries of Greek high culture, people from all over the world flocked to Delphi, not only for the prophecies of the Pythia (which were doubtful and obscure) but especially for the wisdom inscribed in the temple of Phoebus Apollo. But "we are - still - the West" (Ivar Lissner). Therefore, it seems important for us, as educators, to engage with history (if we observe the Austrian and especially German educational scene, it seems that after an unfavorable period of disregarding history, a change in trend is emerging today). The phrase "MnSer Lyav" - "Keep to the measure!" - still applies and is indispensable for us.

# XI/ THE DIFFICULTIES OF THE GIFTED (1982)

Beyond the task of presenting a fascinating issue of diagnosis and therapy in special education, this section has an important role within the entirety of the work: to demonstrate that human existence always carries its difficulties and dangers, that no one gains anything without paying, one could say, with specific burdens. Poets and biographers, who are capable of describing human beings in all their complexity and depth, have consistently depicted how even the most gifted, the most brilliant personalities are still "human beings with their contradictions." This went so far that for certain authors, the "genius and madness" were seen as regularly linked, thus transforming biography into a pathography!

Ultimately, our description in this chapter also aims to counter the prevalent opinion that special education is solely concerned with the care of children with disorders, particularly intellectually deficient children. Such an outlook would significantly narrow the scope of this beautiful scientific discipline. One truly understands the "child" only when comprehending the diversity of their manifestations, while being aware of the inevitable difficulties associated with each form of expression. Yet, these challenges require just as much understanding and assistance as those faced by individuals with intellectual disabilities.

We must also strongly challenge those who too readily employ the term "inferior." The recent periods should have taught us about the profoundly inhumane, even deadly, consequences that this inevitably leads to: the term "unworthy of living" is not far from it! However, those who held such a viewpoint were entirely blind to the fact that they themselves, who regarded themselves racially and characteristically superior, were gravely abnormal individuals, marked by their cold and unreal ideology as well as certain other "psychopathic" traits, and were excluding themselves from the circle of humanity. One of the most powerful figures of that time spoke of "beasts of intelligence" - was he mocking himself? Or, unintentionally, did he inadvertently let slip the truth that high intelligence, when not supported by emotional forces, can be - in our view: causally - linked to dangerous character anomalies? Faced with such life trajectories, which were tragic for many individuals, a fundamental question of psychotherapy emerges, although it is difficult to answer: could early intervention, starting from the outset and recognizing the impending threatening character development along with all its complex causality, have averted the tragedy?

## Suitable - Unsuitable

Intellectually advanced individuals often provoke conflicts early on with their environment, formerly seen as intellectually delayed. The latter adapt fairly well to the given situation through primitive means, functional instincts, and parents believe that everything will develop naturally, even if it's a bit late; they also react quite normally in their social interactions, guided by their instincts. And if certain specific deficits manifest, such as language delay, parents sometimes only realize, for instance upon school entry, that there is a developmental delay (which is tragic as it often means many support opportunities have been missed).

It's different for intellectually precocious individuals. Despite the significant internal difficulties they often encounter, they usually have a spontaneous, above-average activity that they engage in impulsively. They don't recognize imposed behavioral rules; they "must" follow their own path - which often contradicts established rules and leads to conflicts with teachers, of course also with parents and peers.

The children we're discussing in this chapter are not the "compliant" ones who carry out what's asked of them without resistance, who learn obediently without looking left or right, without deviating in the slightest from the prescribed path. Their behavior otherwise is impeccable; their "conduct" grades (in old school reports, it was even referred to in a moralizing jargon as "moral conduct") are excellent. But these "model students" are generally not considered "highly gifted." Folk wisdom has long known that children with good report cards don't always succeed as much in their future lives, while on the other hand, those who later prove to be geniuses were often poor students. However, of course, there are highly gifted individuals who easily satisfy all school requirements and also thrive in their lives. Thus, for us, the concept of high (intellectual) giftedness encompasses logical thinking ability, certainly good linguistic expression, but above all, spontaneity in approaching intellectual problems, autonomous interests, and a critical stance towards others and oneself. (This ability to know oneself - and thus others - inscribed on the pediment of the temple of Apollo at Delphi under the phrase "gnothi sauton" was the origin of the West, even its foundation.) And it's precisely this ability that becomes evident in highly gifted individuals from childhood, through persistent and uncompromising questions, through autonomous and critical experiences undertaken (learning through trial and error according to Dewey).

It's clear that such children are not "easy" and pose significant problems both at home and at school (referred to as "problem children" in Anglo-Saxon literature). Respect for adults, authority, isn't a priority for them. What matters most to them is their own opinion. The two mottos of Theophrastus Paracelsus, "sapere aude!" - "dare to know!" - and "alterius non sit, qui suus esse potest" - "let no one who can be himself belong to another," express this capacity, this intellectual attitude, and it's already present in young children.

## Conflicts

From early childhood and within the family, serious conflicts arise in these children, especially when parents consider the child as their "property," over which they can have control at their discretion, rather than respecting them as autonomous individuals (whom they should guide as long as they are not yet capable of freedom, but also allowing them space as their autonomy emerges). But it's clear that there can be differing opinions - not only verbally, but also in mutual behaviors - about the extent to which a child's autonomy should go.

The manifestations of these conflicts are diverse: from still unreflective but very effective acts of defiance in early childhood, through aggression or a "asthenic" withdrawal in fear and inhibition, to deliberate acts of malice, which are not without danger.

The possibilities for conflict among high-potential children are equally varied in the school setting (which might seem surprising, as such children should have the best chances here!). However, they might not be interested in what the teacher presents and how they do it; sometimes they have their own methods of thinking and working and are unwilling to follow those of the teacher, often expressing this very disrespectfully to the teacher's face. And especially when the teacher is vain, convinced of the perfection of their methods, and incapable of having a conversation with a child, then it's war, a war the child must lose due to disciplinary measures, but that the teacher, who isn't intellectually superior, doesn't win either. If the child's intelligence is truly exceptional, then the child will eventually overcome the conflicts, but much might have been destroyed within them, especially concerning their social behavior capacity.

The attentive reader will have noticed that our description largely corresponds to what was described in the chapter on childhood autism. And indeed, there are relationships. The strong spontaneity of thought and action, good abstraction abilities, autonomous language - all of these have been described here and there; the types of conflicts we described are also found in our "gifted" individuals. If we attempt not to make definitive statements about the typological belonging of "gifted" individuals and differentiate between different autistic subtypes, the disturbance of contact among autistics, the reduced relationships with other people, is the distinguishing criterion. However, it's important to emphasize that the requirements of special education are the same here and there.

## Gifted management

It has been mentioned multiple times in this work that special education, the commitment to children who deviate from the average norm, can teach many things to pedagogy. In this case, the school should demand from the teacher to individualize in all areas; they shouldn't see their task as leading a group of students toward a "common goal" by strictly following the compulsory school curriculum for everyone. Of course, there must be order in teaching, and the teacher should guide the process; the work shouldn't turn into chatter in the classroom. But the teacher can find joy if a child contributes their own input to the content of the teaching, ideas that come to their mind. The teacher will integrate these into their lesson plans, make them fruitful, and also acknowledge a child's original linguistic expressions. In general, the "emerging" language of a gifted child is one of the most delightful things a sensitive person can encounter: the world becomes new in children's language (and one might feel embarrassed about how everyday language, including advertising and political language, has become worn out, even corrupted).

However, the fortunate teacher who has a gifted child in their classroom shouldn't just leave room for their interests and knowledge; they should also strive to encourage them. Because the progress of such a child doesn't solely come from their innate abilities, but from external stimulations that are readily integrated and incorporated into their personality. The author of this contribution fondly recalls the "awakenings" provoked by enthusiastic teachers, as well as the hours spent with peers in the apartment of a certain teacher, engaging in conversations and using the teacher's books - and they know that these experiences are inseparable from the fabric of their destiny.

It is absolutely essential for the teacher to recognize the child's specific gifts and interests (sometimes quite isolated ones), approve of them, and seek to promote them from the perspective of an experienced and committed educator. It's regrettable when such statements from the child (though often expressed with a lot of disrespect) are seen by the teacher as bothersome and disruptive, and they attempt to reduce them "for the sake of classroom discipline." Of course, this might harm a child's spirit - unless a gifted child grows up with such resistances, but who can truly comprehensively understand such complex causalities?

It's clear from what has been said previously that the gifted child benefits from a school capable of good differentiation, one that sets higher demands, otherwise they are under-stimulated, find school boring, don't participate, and their capacities aren't developed as they could be (conversely, less gifted children are often overwhelmed in a school catering to the best, and this can lead to serious discouragement in these children).

Thus, experienced educators have concerns when attempting to "integrate" children who differ too much intellectually into the same class. There's a risk that the class will "level down" ("For everything is the same - yes, because everything is low!" F. Grillparzer in "The Fraternal Strife in Habsburg"). Certainly, in the current sociological situation, it's legitimate to demand equal opportunities for all children and offer them good prospects for advancement. But over time, it has always been shown that the gifted, even the highly gifted, have managed to seize their opportunity, and they've also found their way in an extremely challenging environment.

But regardless of the stance taken on the question of an

integrated or differentiated school from a certain grade level, one thing should be clear: gifted children need a teacher who isn't fixed in routines and strictly defined school programs, a teacher who recognizes the specificity and uniqueness of the child and can interact with them on an intellectual level, who also endures the difficulties such children can cause them in line with the educational law of their personality, and even makes these fruitful for the child, for example by guiding them early on toward self-knowledge and self-critique. For such work, precisely with gifted children, the teacher is richly rewarded: they can experience human creativity, and even foster something so precious. One shouldn't believe that the creative achievements of a younger child must be inferior to those of an older person; they can be just as valid. Here, one is reminded of the profound myth of Pallas Athena, the goddess of intellectual creation: she wasn't born as a helpless infant and didn't grow slowly; no, she sprang forth in full armor, possessing all her strength, from the head of Zeus!

If we have just discussed the importance of creative achievements, we must not forget that in life, especially in relationships with others, it's not only intelligence that matters, but also, equally significantly, human connection, consideration for others, the ability to be "with others," which means emotional and affective values. It's certainly more challenging for the teacher to educate these skills than intellectual abilities. However, they must try, more through lived experience and concrete life examples than through words. As we have already mentioned, the gifted share obvious similarities with autistic children, or undoubtedly belong to this intriguing group of personalities. This emphasizes how difficult it must be to provide "life assistance" in this area of social needs. The teacher should not shy away from this task.

We have extensively addressed the issue of the gifted child in school. This was necessary because it's there that these children's remarkable possibilities first come to the forefront, and where corresponding conflicts arise. What should be done within the family now? The independence, carefree assertion of one's own interests that characterizes this type of child also poses significant challenges in family education, especially if the parents have a similar nature (and from whom else could the child inherit their nature, according to all laws of genetic and social heredity?).

If parents, due to their talents, are successful individuals according to the modern model, there obviously remains little time or motivation to support the gifted child – and yet, tremendous opportunities would be available here, unlike any other social group. Who but the father could address the persistent questions of the child, delving into the depths of human and scientific issues? Who but him could guide the child to nature, museums, their own library? Who wouldn't feel profound joy seeing someone pursue their own path, perhaps with the chance to go even further – if not the father? Modern psychologists have described the dangers that await a "fatherless society"; here, there are as many shortcomings as there are chances and experiences for parents, especially fathers, that are worth it.

Human freedom is a precious good, perhaps the highest in life. We know how rarely it is fully realized, how much it is restricted by critical weakness and a drive "contrary to the law of the spirit." Gifted individuals are the most capable of freedom, but they can also face the most challenging struggles to achieve it. Those called to educate gifted children should strive to assist them in their difficulties with all their might, recognizing and guiding them.

# XII/ ON THE DIFFERENTIAL DIAGNOSIS OF AUTISM (1968)

Around the same time (fall 1943 and early 1944), Leo Kanner of Baltimore and Hans Asperger of Vienna described types of children exhibiting disturbed behaviors. Both chose the term "autistic" to characterize this anomaly ("early infantile autism" and "autistic psychopaths"). This term was not of their own creation, but rather an expression used by Eugen Bleuler, who used it to describe a symptom of schizophrenia. Individuals with schizophrenia withdraw completely (αὐτός, autos) into their own selves, lose contact with reality, no longer engage with the external world, lack initiative, have no specific goals, neglect many aspects of reality, are disorganized, exhibit sudden ideas and strange behaviors, insufficient motivation for numerous individual actions as well as for their overall approach to life, characterized by capriciousness, and simultaneously desiring something and its opposite. Eugen Bleuler, however, didn't solely apply the term "autistic" to mentally ill individuals: when he speaks in his well-known work about "autistic and undisciplined thinking in medicine," he underscores how autistic characteristics are prevalent even in scientific thinking. But he doesn't mention a word about the childhood characteristics of this type.

Interestingly, Kanner and Asperger seemed to consider the term "autism," that is, the restriction of the person and their reactions to their own self, as well as the limitation of reactions and responses to environmental stimuli, as the best designation for the types they wanted to describe. We will see that these are two very different clinical pictures, yet they nevertheless exhibit astonishing similarities in several details.

Since then, a global discussion has emerged on these issues, generating considerable literature, especially in Anglo-Saxon countries and Japan. This literature not only focuses on the etiology and classification of clinical pictures but also on specific psychotherapeutic and educational treatment methods. Initially, this discussion centered solely around children of Kanner's type (Anglo-Saxon authors rarely referring to German-language literature, which is not reciprocated to the same extent). It's the great merit of Van Krevelen to have brought the Asperger type to the attention of Anglo-Saxon authors and to have encouraged comparisons. But even regarding Kanner's "early infantile autism," the matters are far from closed. Difficult differential diagnostic considerations persist, which we will address later.

Concerning the etiology of autism, two opposing viewpoints prevail: the psychogenetic viewpoint and the biological viewpoint. The former, which explains this condition (along with many other developmental disorders) from a psychodynamic perspective, attributes the state to the environmental situation, particularly emotional frustrations. The latter viewpoint attributes this condition to biological and constitutional factors. After thoroughly examining the conflicting arguments, Rimland aligns with the biological etiology, a stance we fully support. The uniformity of the clinical picture, its early formation, concordance in monozygotic twins, and the predominance of boys (about four times as many) point in the same direction, which is hardly explicable by an exogenous etiology stemming solely from the environment or educational situation. Instead, everything suggests a constitutional genesis.

A passionate debate has raged worldwide regarding whether childhood autism is identical to childhood schizophrenia. Generally, Kanner rejected this notion, only considering the possibility that among the "numerous diseases called schizophrenia," autism might be one of them. However, it's worth noting that in the United States, the diagnosis of schizophrenia in children is extremely common and seems to encompass disease trajectories very different from those described in European psychiatric literature, both in terms of etiology and course and prognosis; only recently have voices in the United States begun to call for reflection and limitation.

Rimland extensively examined this question. He strongly argues that early infantile autism is not schizophrenia and that there are numerous differences between the two. Let's simply mention the following: schizophrenia is a process that starts after normal development, in children who were previously entirely normal (which we wouldn't want to affirm for all cases!), and leads to severe dementia - whereas autistic children are atypical from the beginning. From our experience, we add that children who develop schizophrenia in preschool age tend to develop complete language relatively early, which then loses its "communicative character" due to the disease process and eventually disappears more or less completely. We also don't quite agree when Rimland mentions, as an additional distinguishing criterion, that schizophrenic children, unlike autistic ones, have had poor health since birth, exhibit anomalies in breathing, blood circulation, metabolism, motor skills, mild neurological symptoms, show EEG anomalies in 80% of cases, are not "solitary," but tend to be intrusive and seek contact - we rather think that cases described in this manner are an extension of the concept of schizophrenia, which we find inappropriate, and that these are rather children with organic brain disorders, who may indeed exhibit symptoms sometimes reminiscent of "functional psychosis." On the other hand, we fully agree on the criteria that schizophrenics are filled with severe and irrational anxiety, and that children, at times, exhibit hallucinatory symptoms or at least ones that can be inferred (for example, from the "hallucinatory gaze").

Furthermore, there is a concordant heredity in cases of schizophrenia, which is not the case in autistic children - however, we think we can deduce enough from Kanner's publications and those of his students to support a hereditary origin of "early infantile autism," as we would also argue for cases we have observed of the Kanner type (with very similar characteristics as described by Kanner, but with evident autistic traits).

Distinguishing between the state described by Kanner and personality disorders due to organic brain processes is equally challenging. Kanner himself and his students (like Eisenberg) always emphasized that early infantile autism was a very rare disorder, warning against "widening" and "diluting" the diagnosis, and wishing to exclude cases with clear cerebral organic etiology from their diagnosis.

It is true that we do find children with behavioral disorders resulting from prenatal, peri- or postnatal cerebral disorders, especially after early encephalitis, who astonishingly resemble the early infantile autism type in many ways, but who also exhibit more or less evident signs of cerebral disorders.

We find the typical "expressive manifestations" that easily

allow recognizing autistic behaviors (often overlooked by Americans): the "absent" gaze, turned inwards, paying little attention to people in the environment, poor facial expression, all the typical features of speech described by Kanner (here again, we would like to add that, as a general rule, expressive qualities of speech are also unusual - monotony or anomalies in intonation, speech melody).

In subjects with cerebral disorders exhibiting autistic traits, there are significant differences in intellectual level, sometimes even severe intellectual impairment. However, very diverse intellectual levels are also present in children with "early infantile autism." It is certain that in subjects with organic disorders, one can often observe psychological characteristics considered typical of "cerebral dysfunction," such as form perception disorders; however, this doesn't apply to all cases. In all cases of autistic behavior, however, it's necessary to carefully evaluate all elements that might argue for or against an organic cause: detailed prenatal, peri- and postnatal history, searching for even minor neurological symptoms (examination programs have become very extensive recently, including postural and posture reflexes), encephalography and particularly EEG. Nor should the examination of hereditary metabolic anomalies ("inborn errors of metabolism") be neglected, as many disorders of this kind, including phenylketonuria, are accompanied by severe autistic symptoms, complete withdrawal from reality.

For a long time, we have noticed a fact: even in cases where it has been proven with certainty or a strong likelihood that an organic cause was behind autistic behavior, distinctive autistic traits were also present in ancestors, especially in fathers. This strongly suggests that there must be a constitutional predisposition to react in an autistic manner, which is then "highlighted" or even exaggerated by cerebral disorder. We will come back to this fact later.

Additionally, Destunis recently presented that there are often psychoses similar to schizophrenia based on organic brain lesions - an observation entirely parallel to the above.

Early infantile autism must also be differentiated from states of mental retardation. However, as we have already explained, it is common for children with brain-based mental retardation to also exhibit autistic traits and thus more or less completely manifest the clinical picture of autism. On the other hand, Kanner's types, if they do not develop language, also end up with profound mental impairment.

Nevertheless, "early autistics" are clearly distinct from cases of "ordinary" mental retardation: they do not exhibit the frequent physical deformities found in mentally retarded individuals, the apathy in gaze and facial expression, but are generally attractive and display great skill when they wish to (unlike the often impaired motor skills of mentally retarded individuals). When their interest and activity are focused, they also show unique mnemonic capabilities, special aptitudes, for example in the musical domain (for instance, a child who does not develop language possesses a rich repertoire of complex melodies).

Autistic behavior must also be differentiated from deaf-mutism. Parents often consider this because these children seem to be "disconnected" from many external stimuli, including auditory stimuli. In reality, deaf children, lacking such an important "contact tool" as hearing, often exhibit behavioral difficulties similar to autistic behavior: carefree aggressiveness, resistance to demands (and it appears they do not "want" to understand). However, for an experienced professional, the distinction between a deaf child and an autistic child is not difficult, aside from specific auditory tests: it turns out that the autistic child sometimes reacts to noises or sounds (which is not the case with a deaf child). Above all, the deaf child actively seeks human contact through means other than hearing; they have an expressive gaze, an overly lively and expressive facial expression, they "communicate" with others in a very vibrant manner, and are fundamentally different from the autistic child, who is not interested in any of that. - Of course, there are also "complex" children who exhibit both neurological and auditory disorders, as well as autistic traits in their behavior. This then poses very complex diagnostic problems.

Next, we will delve into the discussion between Asperger's autistic behavior type and Kanner's.

If Kanner's early infantile autism is a state close to psychosis, or even psychotic (although not identical to childhood schizophrenia), the "core cases" of Asperger are extremely intelligent children, endowed with exceptional spontaneity and originality of thought, with particular abilities in logic and abstraction - even if they can sometimes have more or less "bewildering" thinking, that is, they follow their own path, indifferent to reality (much like paranoid thinking, albeit in a pathological manner, is strictly logical but disconnected from reality); in this context, it's also worth noting that these children are not so much concerned with the richness of the world as they are with specialized interests that are often very unusual and impractical. Another important difference from early infantile autism is the fact that the mentioned types develop very early (often before walking freely) a perfect, grammatically elevated language, highly precise, with independent "embryonic" expressions, created on the spot (which may sometimes resemble schizophrenic neologisms). However, it should be noted from the outset that the language of these children shares with that of Kanner's types, which is so imperfect, the fact that its primary goal is not to create interpersonal relationships or to "communicate" something to others, but rather to express themselves autonomously, to give voice to their spontaneous interests, without showing consideration or adaptation to the listener, both in expressive manifestations and in content.

Given that these children develop at a much higher personality level than Kanner's types, it's understandable that they pose more significant conflicts and become the subject of medical observation later, around the middle of early childhood. However, with hindsight, it can be recognized that they seem marked by their distinctiveness from the very beginning of their lives, much like the other type. Furthermore, we believe we have sufficient indications to assert that this is an innate, even hereditary, characteristic of a personality, which strictly corresponds to the definition of psychopathy, even though we admit that the formative influences of parents of similar nature may be important (but they alone cannot explain the condition).

As the disorder in "our" children is far less severe than in early autistics, it is also understandable that the social prognosis is much better. Even though they are in constant conflict, especially during their childhood and schooling, they follow their own path with marked spontaneity and originality, without being diverted and with an almost surreal confidence. They often gravitate towards eccentric scientific or artistic professions, sometimes with capabilities bordering on genius. It even appears that for certain exceptional scientific or artistic performances, a dose of "autism" is almost necessary: a certain detachment from concrete and practical reality, a focus on a specific domain worked on with powerful dynamics and great originality, sometimes verging on eccentricity, a restriction or deviation from affective relationships with other human beings.

Although these two types differ in their intellectual level and personality level, similarities in essential aspects and subtle details are nonetheless observed; undoubtedly, it's these similarities that led both authors to independently choose the same name to express the nature of the disorder. When Kanner tries to describe this nature using the terms "innate phenomenon of a particular deficit in the formation of affective contacts," it also applies to Asperger's types.

All authors who have attempted to describe and interpret these children have made similar statements about the nature of the disorder. Asperger speaks of a deficit in the affective ("thymic") region of the personality (and also deduces disturbance in interpersonal relationships as well as abnormal sexual behaviors); Van Krevelen speaks of a disturbance in "intuitive" capacities (which, according to his description, means the same thing); the same interpretation is found in Friedemann: autism is a disturbance of development in the dynamic domain of personality, an alienation (in the sense of depth psychology). In-depth interpretations of autism by J. Lurz go in the same direction: it is a disturbance of the self's structure, a weakness of the self, a lack of personality integrity. Bosch also describes it as a state of weakness, speaking of an absence or delay in the constitution of a distinct and common world. All these ultimately so similar criteria are common to both types of autistic behavior.

But the similarities go even further, down to subtle details. First, there are correspondences in expressive manifestations, the peculiarities of gaze and facial expression, which we have already mentioned are found both in children with organic brain disorders and in classic Kanner's types. But the same can be found in Asperger's children. Even in the children we have described, who are much more organized, there are movement stereotypies, activity restriction in the form of stereotypy, for example, a fetishistic fixation on a particular toy, a fixation on a specific environmental situation (which is why autistic children experience extremely difficult and enduring homesickness when they change environments, precisely because they cannot root themselves in a new situation with the sense that normal children can have in the presence of a new situation and different people).

A curious trait that we have often observed in children with early infantile autism as well as in "our" children is their inclination to spin objects that do not seem at all suited for it—coins, building blocks, and even chairs—with exceptional skill, visibly manifesting great satisfaction in this rotational movement. This is also an example of the fact that these children, who are generally clumsy or even markedly apraxic, are capable of particular dexterous performances when their emotion drives them to do so.

Similarities in the linguistic domain are also remarkable—both in expressive manifestations and in the "thymic" qualities of speech (we have also discussed this previously). But there are also content-related similarities: what Kanner rightly highlighted as particularly typical of his autistic children is that they learn very late, or perhaps never, to use the pronoun "I" (instead of referring to themselves as "he" or "you"; he calls this "pronominal inversion"). This is often observed in "our" children as well, who are, however, much more developed, which testifies to the fact that these types are "disintegrated," that they have no anchoring within themselves! There is also a tendency toward stereotypical use of certain terms (once again, almost "fetishistic"!).

In general, language anomalies clearly reveal the nature of autism, namely the inability to develop interpersonal relationships stemming from the depths of the soul ("affective contacts," according to Kanner): language, no matter the diversity of its level, does not have so much of a "communicative" character. It does not appear as a supreme human tool, this "zoon politikon," to find the way to the other, but rather as a stereotypy, like an empty movement, like so many other things in autistics. It is the expression of spontaneous impulses, the expression of internal, albeit highly original, problems that are very one-sided. So, when the autistic child speaks, they neither seek nor need a listener; even if they speak very intelligently, they have absolutely no idea whether it would be better to speak in a given situation or whether it would be preferable to "let silence be golden"; they also don't need to be heard, they "resonate" without taking that into account!

Ultimately, after our reflections, we are faced with an astonishing fact: "autistic behaviors" can describe behavioral disorders of various origins, which can indeed be distinguished and must be, but nonetheless present great similarities in their overall character.

But we want to go even further. We believe that exhibiting

"autistic behaviors" is a general possibility of human existence. Certainly, it is deeply ingrained in human beings to be "interpersonal": long before their intellectual capacities develop, that is, from early childhood, the human child has differentiated contact capabilities; they are capable of producing expressions (as L. Klages brilliantly emphasizes) (with gaze and facial expressions, gestures and vocalizations) and perceiving the expressive manifestations of others (thus, they understand the affective aspect of language long before they can grasp the "intellectual meaning of words"); they are dynamically oriented towards others (R. Spritz describes this very impressively as "finding an object," although we have reservations about categorizing such personal empathy as an "object relation").

However, humans are not just a part of the world, resonating with beings and things, in some way a function of the respective situation. They are also a "Self," distinct from the environment. There are developmental phases where this is particularly strongly manifested: certain phases of anxiety in young children, especially adolescence, which can lead to serious conflicts with the environment, deep turmoil for educators. Certain experiences can also turn the individual inwards, make them "autistic" in a certain way—disappointments, intense sufferings, for example; the expressive manifestations and the individual's experience in depression show great similarities with autism. Lastly, humans also behave in an "autistic" way in states of spontaneous mental creation and activity, as they must protect themselves largely from the external world, from humans and things, both externally and internally—this can be illustrated by numerous examples in poetic descriptions, visual arts (as in Rembrandt's case),

186

and caricature. Thus, we must recognize, by adopting the principle "nothing human is alien to us," that it is generally possible for humans to behave in an autistic manner!

Under pathological circumstances—whether due to brain disease, predisposition, certainly also in interaction with abnormal environmental stimuli—pathological degrees of autism can develop, the extreme of which is psychosis, schizophrenia, or the severely abnormal state of "early infantile autism."

In this work, only the issue of differential diagnosis has been addressed, not the description and interpretation of clinical pictures, nor etiology (it should be noted only that Kanner regards the cause of early infantile autism as a "mystery"). For these issues, we refer to the abundant literature.

# XIII/ WHAT PEDAGOGY CAN LEARN FROM MEDICINE (1980)

The speech by Karl Wolf in Salzburg in 1974, titled "Natura magistra" - "Nature as the Teacher," remains vividly etched in my memory, and many of you, faithful participants in our conferences, will also have the same recollection. Yes, I would like to consider this concept as the motto of our gatherings: we must follow nature in all its diversity, including the spiritual realm within the human "nature," when we, this circle of educators, wish to discuss our tasks. We must remain true to nature, I say, not overly reducing things conceptually, for that can easily lead to extravagances.

Nature includes - and this is what I will elaborate on before you today - what is extraordinary, outside the norm, what is pathological, diseased. If we recognize this and draw conclusions for education, then we understand the human being and can adapt to them.

It is not easy to define what health and disease truly are. Is health a statistical norm - and disease what deviates from it? But life is never in equilibrium, situated in the middle of the Gaussian curve, it lives through oppositions, oscillates around them, sometimes extremely so in extreme situations, influenced by internal and external factors, to thereby be better prepared for them. "Equilibrium" would be entropy, death through cold. But, looked at differently, is disease a defect, an organ loss, a functional failure? Or does it belong to the life of each one of us?

If we seek to understand life more deeply, we realize that its oscillations always lie at the edges of failure, that we constantly challenge failure to be fully aware of life in all its intensity: the mountaineer who lives in the thinnest air, at the edge of tolerance, the ascetic who pushes themselves physically and mentally to the extreme limits - and the patient who guards the flame of life until their final breath.

Thus, it can be said that fragility is part of human nature, not perfection - to demand the latter would be a utopia, an impossibility. This is precisely what can be said about the famous request of the World Health Organization that every individual should enjoy the highest possible standard of physical, mental, and social health, and that this should be achieved, organized, perhaps by this great anonymous entity to which one would only need to submit. But isn't it the prevailing general dissatisfaction today, largely due to the increasingly present feeling of the inhumanity of such "health organization"?

However, an undeniable biological truth is as follows: a person's qualities and difficulties, their particular capabilities and their clearly pathological traits go hand in hand, mutually condition each other, they are inseparable; it is not possible to simply treat what is pathological. It is precisely the gifted individual who must also face a high degree of vulnerability and suffering. The personal history of all great minds is proof of this.

Great minds were always aware of this, and here are a few quotes on this subject: "Ah, now I recognize that nothing perfect is granted to man," Faust complains. And the poignant poem by Mörike, precisely in its naivety: "I carry my cross and my sufferings / I write them with chalk / and whoever has no cross and sufferings / let them erase my rhymes!" - but they remain indelible! And finally: "Steal the light from the snake's throat!" (Romanian Journal by Hans Carossa) - torn from the snake, without it, there would be no light; the snake, suffering, and danger as prerequisites for excellence - that is human existence. From there, we come to ideas about "beauty in pathology" (title of an unforgettable lecture by the pathologist Marsch) - not without danger, considering that this can encompass essential tendencies of modern art, as well as all their disguises, ugliness, and pathology being elevated to a cult.

However, we must stick to the ancient correspondence of beauty, goodness, and truth, but we must not reduce the notion of beauty to what is merely pretty, pleasant, and petty. It seems to me that it's precisely the educator who should know these connections. They should talk to the young and tell them what it means to be human. Proof of this can be found in all poets, generally in all artists. Schiller, a great interpreter of human existence, beautifully expressed it: "You share knowledge with elevated spirits, / art, oh human, is yours!" - elevated spirits, pure spirits, angels, cannot have art, it only comes from human frailty, from their capacity to suffer, from the inclusion of the "pathological"! This is what the educator must teach and live. By doing so, they counteract the frightening trend of the "movement of time," of the "course of time," where in a person's life, comfort and the capacity for enjoyment are the only ideals, where consciousness, if not abolished, is nonetheless reduced because consciousness is uncomfortable. Children are killed in the womb without scruples (they have "arrived" when only pleasure was sought - and now, responsibility must be taken?). We harden our hearts to the suffering of others and to hunger in the world. And yet, the understanding of suffering should lead us, ourselves, into our own depths (knowing oneself is the great goal of Western man, from the times of the Apollo at Delphi, who inscribed this requirement - "gnothi seauton" - on the front of his temple), and it should also motivate us to help our fellow human beings. We will develop this further. What deviates from the norm is easier to recognize than what is "normal." This is how the school of contemplation should begin, which every educator must go through. The average norm does not strike us, we recognize the essence in it. We do not notice the average norm, we recognize the essence in it. To students aspiring to understand human beings, we give the following instruction: seek what is different from expectation, and from there, from the "striking" appearance, delve into depth, seek what the spirit and soul express in that apparent image! Seek precisely what deviates from the norm; can the structural law of this child's personality be recognized? By understanding this, in a very individual way, by distancing ourselves from the notion of norm, the construction of a person, we also understand the difficulties and conflicts of the child with their environment, and as educators, we can contribute to mastering and resolving these conflicts. Thus, my explanations fit into the general issue of this conference. This must now be exemplified. It is very revealing to note a contradiction between a child's chronological age and their actual impression of age; it is not so much the size that matters as other delays in maturation: a delay in teething is already quite well known and rightly taken into account when assessing a child's school maturity (at the time of school entry, the incisors should already have been largely replaced!). This criterion is not so coincidental: if one considers that the skin - and teeth are appendages of the skin - is formed from the outer germ layer, the ectoderm, just like the central nervous system, that teeth and the nervous system are linked in terms of development, it is not surprising to find parallels in the maturation rhythm. But there are also other criteria for delays in maturation: proportions of the body outline and facial shapes, as Wilfried Zeller has described so well, but also psychological criteria: the immediacy of infantile and childlike contact, revealed in an open view of the world; the child has not yet learned to distance themselves, just as they have not yet acquired the distance of abstraction, objective work. From this arise typical conflicts because the school's demand and the child's capabilities do not match. Physical and psychological infantilism is not only important at school entry age: if the delay in maturation persists, problems with work (sometimes despite good intelligence), and deficiencies in social integration persist.

And the most tragic thing: juvenile delinquency is often correlated with character infantilism. Why is the example mentioned above so significant? Unlike any other living creature, humans consciously live in time, experience time. "Time, yours - man's true sacrament," Josef Weinheber says in his calendar maxims "O man, pay attention!" But the regularity of maturation is part of the issue of time, especially for a child. If it's disrupted - in the sense of infantilism or, much more rarely, precocity - difficult-to-master conflicts and problems of direction arise. A second example: from the earliest times, probably since humans began to reflect on themselves, the recognition that there are different instances of nervous and psychic regulation: consciousness and will (which we partly share with animals, thus called the "animal nervous system") - and the "vegetative" life (shared with the plant kingdom), which governs metabolic and circulatory regulations, but also includes unconscious processes, affective processes ("thymic"). This also has much to do with a person's fundamental mood, with the ability to cling to the world "with clinging organs" (Faust). Disorders of mental life, conflicts experienced with our environment, are reflected in disturbances of vegetative functions - and are recognizable by such symptoms, they become so obvious - precisely in human expressive manifestations that we share with animals - these are paths of knowledge of "comparative behavior research," it also allows us to live with animals, to understand and love them. Vegetative manifestations occur involuntarily and consciously - they cannot deceive if only understood, they can also be "fabricated" to deceive. They are sensitive seismographs of psychic processes for those who know how to observe. Another ancient name for the vegetative is also the "sympathetic" nervous system, the one that sympathizes, that feels with, that connects the bodily to the psychic, the mental to the somatic, uniting them into a single person who, thanks to these processes, becomes recognizable and accessible to others, enabling them to engage with others.

Thus, it is the vegetative manifestations that reveal the feelings, affections, and emotions that occur within a person at a given moment: processes at the level of blood vessels (such as blushing or paling of the skin), glands (tears, brightness or opacity of the gaze), muscles (motor movements, even tics), "shared feelings" which also have their typical expressions. What we have said so far must be extended in two directions: it's not only about momentary emotions that unfold at the level of the vegetative system but also about attitudes - and also about poor attitudes - that deeply permeate the child's life, strongly interfering with the motivation process. For example, one can mention nervous concentration disorders, so frequent and so determinant for the child's school fate. Intellectual talent can be normal or even above average (and children excel in exciting and stimulating tests) - but there's a lack of the necessary "cohesion" for working in school and even in homework situations at home, the ability to properly channel the incoming sensory impressions, to protect oneself from disturbances and distractions; children are incapable of "active attention," leading to downtime and a sense of helplessness. The combination with other vegetative symptoms, some of which we've listed, indicates the path of diagnosis, but direct observation of the working behavior of these children also guides educators to recognize the existing disorder. Given that many school destinies and thus life destinies of children are determined by these conflicts, a strong involvement from the educators of these children is necessary, as well as good collaboration between doctors and psychologists, the latter having developed effective concentration training methods in combination with general people management techniques. And a second point, already implied in what has just been said: vegetative functions are not only at play in the waves of momentary affects but also express fundamental dispositions, enduring attitudes of personality: psychic oppression, whether caused from within or without, or fear that goes beyond situation-conditioned fear, or fear that is inscribed in every human being as an important regulator, even as the "beginning of wisdom," which is already situated in the pathological domain, or finally, a deficit of vitality inherent in the personality or resulting from constant deprivation on the physical or psychological plane, but manifesting recognizably in attitude and tonus (tension, also metaphorically), or even in the structure and function of all organs (because the "trophic" growth of organs is also controlled by the vegetative system!). Psychic processes can be primarily and particularly recognized through vegetative signs. Nature has given us the capacity to recognize them instinctively, intuitively, initially unconsciously (and this capacity is shared with animals as well, especially those accustomed to living with us).

But it's also necessary to make these sources of knowledge conscious, to record and systematize them. However, precisely at this moment when the "pallor of thought" sneaks in, the danger arises of intellectualizing, of posing questions, of misinterpreting - and thus making mistakes. Such self-critique from the educator, constant self-doubt, is necessary to avoid falling into these errors! However, note this: the recognition and understanding of vegetative processes, especially when they verge on the extreme and pathological, are an important source of personality diagnosis. What manifests before our eyes leads us, as educators, into the child's inner self; it takes us to the threshold of understanding the conflicts at play here. But when, finally, vegetative symptoms improve, such as the "organic neurosis" that tormented the child and the parents, we also have the assurance of having helped the child, the child as a whole. After the pathology of maturation and that of vegetative processes, a third area of abnormal behavior will be addressed: the pathology of child contact. Being human, being able to relate to others, is an existential capacity of a human being from a very young age. For this, the child is richly endowed by nature, which is part of their innate heritage, their instinct. But this is also necessary: a lack, a deprivation in this area is one of the most serious damages that can be inflicted on a young child. Thus, from the very beginning, the child needs, for their survival, caresses and cuddles, maternal looks and words (not the sense of the words of their language, which they will only understand much later). Recent research (though some remains hypothetical) has shown that this is absolutely necessary for the child's development, especially in the first few days, even the first few hours after birth. And from the very start, the child is also capable of "responding" to these human and maternal stimuli (which are truly "key stimuli" in the sense of comparative behavior research) - through vocalizations as varied as they are individual, ranging from impressive cries to gazes and smiles, the first signs of intentional attention to others. This intensifies rapidly and individualizes into a fascinating play, unfolding simultaneously with self-awareness and personality formation: at three months, the baby responds indiscriminately to all faces, even artificial attraction, and smiles at them; from around five months, the baby starts to "stranger," to clearly differentiate the familiar and beloved person (the mother) from the stranger, to fear and reject (unless the latter gains the child's trust and attention through intelligent behavior). This further differentiates into a wonderful interplay between individuals, where personal space, attraction and repulsion, familiarity and fear, leading and being led, intertwine and unfold; this expresses both the child's inimitable individuality and the distillate of all their previous experiences. This is a peculiar phenomenon that wasn't included in the domain of older child psychology, neither the concept of "contact" nor its pathology (probably because this discipline was too intellectually structured, while these phenomena occur on a different level than the intellectual).

However, today the disorders of personal contact are attracting worldwide interest. (You surely know that I myself am involved in this development.) An already substantial scientific literature deals with "infantile autism" (the term "autism" meaning turned inwards, self-centered (autos), centered on one's own self; the first two authors, Leo Kanner and Hans Asperger, referred to this condition. Although the images described by the two authors differ in etiology and phenomenology, there are nevertheless striking similarities in behavior. It is not the place here to comprehensively examine the fascinating issue of infantile autism. It is sufficient to mention that such a limitation of human relationships inevitably plunges these children into serious conflicts with their environment. They don't understand what the human world expects of them - and they don't do it, instead constantly violating the unwritten and written laws that have always governed this behavior.

The "central trap" of the type I've described shows a strong spontaneity in thought and action, a special talent for abstraction, for independent critical thinking that avoids predefined paths and seeks its own ways, which sometimes venture into the absurd. But the world demands that they react correctly, that they learn what is presented to them, that they conform. However, they cannot and do not want to do so. With incredible insolence, they confront their parents and teachers, debate with them, without respecting the wisdom of their elders.

The "holy wrath" of the educator does not bend them, much

less the layman! They even profit from it, finding it interesting to irritate the educator. It becomes an interesting object of keen psychological observation.

The behavior of intelligent autistic children (in our country, almost exclusively boys) is significant evidence for our thesis stated above: that the advantages and difficulties of a child are inseparably linked, that this must be respected, that one cannot eliminate one and leave the other. But if you adapt to their peculiarities, if you play with them, or even identify with them, if you also explain to their group (for example, as a teacher of the class) the particularities of these children, you mitigate conflicts with them, give them a place in the community by allowing them to showcase their exceptional qualities. And even though emotionally reaching autistic children is challenging, when they feel understood, bonds can nonetheless be established that last a lifetime.

Dear listeners, I have shared a bit from my workshop, that of a child psychiatrist passionate about education. What was the purpose? Certainly not to turn you into medical enthusiasts or lead you to unconditional acceptance of my way of thinking. That would be futile. Nor is it about creating a system of childhood psychopathology that can be learned from descriptions.

But how does one learn from a teacher - the young person just entering the education profession, but also the experienced one who is aware that they must "always strive to improve," that one learns nowhere, especially not in relationships with human beings? In the last meeting of the "Club of Rome," here in Salzburg, it was postulated that "creative learning" was an important way to overcome the deep crisis of our time. I would interpret it as follows: one looks at the construction of another's thought from their own point of view (- oh, if only one could firmly root oneself there!), confronts it with what has grown within as experience; then, the process of creative appropriation must come into play, which means making a decision; not a form of adoption, of taking that on, which is stealing, but rather recognizing what is similar and what is different. "What the other has recognized hasn't struck me yet, they're right, I thank them for that!" "No, but now that the other says it this way, I realize my own position is correct and not theirs; I must distance myself critically from it!" All of this, however, must be constantly confronted with vigilant self-doubt, with a clear consciousness of one's own potential for error. In the process of knowledge, nothing is more dangerous than too high a sense of certainty, the belief that everything one thinks and says is definite, a danger that grows with the passing years: it's called "experience," and one sets - and thus narrows oneself, depriving oneself of the capacity to learn. Thus, in retrospect, one can say the following: the ability to say something valid even at an advanced age depends on the ability to maintain this process of creative appropriation I've tried to talk about. And what the old woman says to the young girl about love (in Mörike), it also holds true in matters of science: "I was young, I can also speak about it. I've grown old, that's why my words matter!"

What was hidden between the lines in what has been said so far must now be dealt with in a bit more detail: how to move from diagnosis, recognition of troubles and difficulties, from the cause of conflicts to the proper management of conflicts, so that the child can realize themselves in this world?

I believe it must remain undeniable that the therapeutic approach should not be based on deduced principles, but on the understanding of the individual child's person, their peculiarities, and also their abnormal characteristics arising from disposition and lived history. The conflicts that persist, or even worsen, which hinder positive developments and can lead to secondary damage (what is called neuroticization), mostly result from not recognizing what the child is expressing, in the language of their organs and in their overall behavior.

I've provided some examples of pathology above. The following must indicate how conflicts resulting from these can be "overcome," as far as possible for human beings and their environment. It must also show that one should not be too easily satisfied, not content with apparent causalities.

Conflicts resulting from maturation anomalies are inevitable if, for instance, the delay in maturation, especially psychological maturation, is not properly considered. Overloading the child - for example, sending a child to school too early - is inevitable, secondary neuroticization with "psychosomatic" symptoms, severe behavioral difficulties (like dangerous aggression), as well as anxiety and despair, can be the consequence. A delay in school entry, certainly with intensive care of the child in the preschool group or in a preschool class, can indeed solve the problem, offer important maturation stimuli, and enable normal further development.

However, this perspective does not always go far enough. There are cases where a more severe maturation deficit hides behind an apparent delay in maturation: a deprivation of favorable stimuli (for instance, because the mother, serving the fetish of a certain standard of living, believes she must pursue a profession) or a severe disturbance that children undergo due to conflicts in the disintegrating marriage of parents and due to the ongoing battle even after separation, with the child often used as a weapon, manipulated against the former partner. Such a situation - which I have encountered often - indeed seems capable of exerting an inhibitory influence on the maturation of the personality, both for the present and for the entire lifespan granted to a human being: a persistent defect remains that - in the sense of A. Portmann's "social transmission" - labels such a person as unfinished, not free, incapable of making decisions. This is where the limits of empathetic assistance and psychotherapeutic approaches are also evident: no decision, no matter how understandable from a guardian's perspective, no advice, no matter how well-intentioned from a child psychiatrist expert, can prevent the parent who "possesses" the child at that moment from continuing to poison the child's soul with hatred towards the other parent; and one cannot always rely on time, which acts patiently yet inexorably and eventually sets things right when the child finally matures and thinks for themselves - not always, I say, sometimes the damage remains incurable.

As a second example, I described vegetative dysfunctions, along with some behavioral disorders and conflicts stemming from them. Once again, several therapeutic approaches would need to be mentioned, ranging from suggestive therapy for certain "organic neuroses" (if cured, the existing conflict situation can sometimes calm down), to psychologically based treatment methods for concentration disorders, play therapy, "creativity training." But here too, it's important to stress that things should not be oversimplified, both in terms of diagnosis and in terms of treatment: even if an organic symptom disappears through suggestive treatment, severe family tension may still be the cause of symptomatology, and such "revelatory therapy" (as depth psychologists have mocked such methods) merely masks the problem without truly resolving it.

It is easier to understand that, in the case of character peculiarities (like the described contact disorders), understanding the child, accepting them, and engaging with them is immediately useful. The autistic boy is no longer the strange, the outsider in the world, the aggressions of others that pursue the "ugly duckling" openly challenge him - the teacher has shown others that the one ostracized by the crowd excels in mathematics, understands thinking problems better, can assess people better on a psychological level: and now he has his place in the group, others come to him and ask him for help with tasks, even tolerating his professor-like behavior ("Doctor of Sciences"). But if only every teacher recognized the benefits of the problematic child ("problem child") instead of thinking of them as a burden to the class!

What has been presented here through individual examples must now be formulated in a general and recapitulative manner. We are all engaged in the grand process of education, which makes the child a free and responsible human being, destined to achieve self-knowledge and social commitment. As educators, we must let ourselves be guided by nature, sharpen our gaze for peculiarities, for what is out of the ordinary, for tensions and contradictions. It is precisely these contradictions - individual and among individuals - that construct the social structure and confer value to each individual. Already two and a half thousand years ago, at the dawn of the Western world, a great philosopher of nature, Heraclitus, expressed it: "The opposite is in accord, the most beautiful harmony arises from what is different in itself." This means that the pathological should not offend the aesthete's gaze: it is part of the image of reality and ultimately builds its harmony. And the pathological should not offend the moralist's gaze either: it is a part of the human condition, it is our destiny - and it propels us toward perfection.

I mentioned earlier that the gaze must be sharpened. But how is that done? One must observe patiently, gaze, to the extent that acquired vision surpasses innate sight. It's about understanding connections, integrating contradictions and anomalies into the picture, maintaining things in a precarious balance through rigorous self-critique of one's methodology. The patience with which people are observed must also be accompanied by respect for the other person, including the child: one must take what they say seriously - and also what they conceal (though it can be beneficial for the child to help them understand what is hidden through empathetic questions - the legitimate method of psychoanalysis).

If the educator matures such knowledge and puts it into practice, they will make fewer pedagogical mistakes, be better capable of "forming" immature children as "representatives of life" (Romano Guardini). But the pursuit of an insightful perspective also brings a rich reward to the educator themselves.

May I allow myself to quote here the magnificent words of perfection from the mouth of Lynceus the lookout? - for we all aspire, you and I, the young and the old, on the path of our educator profession, toward perfection. So now:

Born to see,

Destined to gaze,

I have sworn an oath to the tower,

The world pleases me.

I look far,

I see up close,

The moon and the stars,

The forest and the deer.

Thus, in everything I see

The eternal beauty,

And as it pleases me,

I also find pleasure.

Happy eyes,

Whatever they have seen,

Whether it is as it should be,

It was still so beautiful!

# XIV/ KANNER AUTISM (1982)

## Occurrence, first impressions

At first glance, autistic children are so striking that one would think that such types can hardly go unnoticed. Yet, they were once described under the label of "moral insanity" even in the German medical literature. Kanner believed that early childhood (or infantile) autism was extraordinarily rare. However, based on the now available case reports, it must be assumed that there is about 1 infantile autistic child for every 5000 infants, with admitted differences in severity. However, one must not make the mistake of diagnosing very mentally retarded children or those exhibiting symptoms of neurological impairment as infantile autistic children. Most of these cases are only presented to the physician starting from the second or third year of life, but mothers retrospectively describe that the child was already remarkable from early childhood: they did not show the fine signs of human affection, which develop abundantly in the first months of life, the interaction of gazes, facial expressions, and sounds, which constituted an essential part of the mother-child dyad, was missing, so that the child seemed to be a true stranger in the world. And it remained so. Kanner defined the disorder as "an innate phenomenon of a particular handicap in the formation of affective contact." The initial impression is that no matter what you propose to these children to encourage them to participate, they may respond with irritation and ill will. They play in a strange and monotonous manner with themselves and a few objects. There is no activity that serves to cope with the respective environmental situation; rather, what happens consists of stereotypes, automatic and uniform movements, and purposeless manipulation of objects. Learning progress is often not visible for many months, reinforcing the impression of imbecility. However, it is the unsettling gaze, which does not turn toward others, the expressionless facial expression, the lack of facial response to painful stimuli, that make these children, even at first glance, give the impression of being strangers and explain that any emotional intensity in them is denied with the term "moral insanity."

## Symptomatology and diagnosis

However, it's not just the lack of contact with parents, acquaintances, and doctors that characterizes these children, but they also show emotional reactions whenever the child's physical environment changes. Every change of bed, every new bed (with an increase in body length), for example, a new song on a record, and similar things are met with panic; extreme sensitivity to changes in the child's material environment is talked about, which contrasts strangely with insensitivity towards strangers. Thus, infantile autistic children feel reasonably comfortable only in the spaces and among the toys to which they are accustomed, making it difficult to admit them to children's hospitals or adolescent psychiatric services or foster homes. Even toys must always be the same; their favorite record must be played over and over again; it's hard to present them with a different one, which is a torment for parents and caregivers. Their play is never constructive. Favorite pastime: "going around in circles," turning the faucet, watching water flow and splash. Another almost bizarre "family" similarity shown by infantile autistic children among themselves is the preference for spinning objects, coins, building blocks, even things that don't seem suitable at all, but they can set them spinning with incredible dexterity. It's hard to say what fascinates the children so much about this activity: the stereotype? the flickering of moving bodies? the experience of a rotating body emerging from the surface? One can even use the demonstration of such a game to establish a sort of contact with severely disturbed Kanner children. Central problems concern whether such a child is not mentally retarded after all and how to enable them to learn language through remedial educational measures. Children who don't play meaningfully, who don't express themselves linguistically, and who don't respond to adult efforts are regularly considered retarded, and they also do not cooperate with intelligence tests. Follow-up studies show that these children often make significant progress between the ages of 5 and 7, but they remain autistic and often must be seen as mentally disabled or mildly mentally disabled in their abilities. The highest form of human communication is language. A severely autistic child, withdrawn into themselves, doesn't need language: they have nothing to communicate to others! If it stays with this mutism, then the future fate of these children is sad: efforts to educate them in any useful activity are sought in vain, they remain dependent on care in appropriate institutions. However, if the children's interest is aroused and language develops through sustained remedial education and the provision of materials, the overall prognosis for their lives improves significantly. Some children become suitable for school and eventually become somewhat socializable. Kanner was the first to describe that infantile autistic children are capable of using language from the age of

3. And even though the children make great progress in terms of speech, they learn to use the pronoun "I" very late, or even never, but systematically use "you" instead. These children are not at home in themselves, says Asperger. It is quite characteristic of infantile autistic children that, instead of giving an answer, they always repeat the question or sentence of the adult addressing them ("echolalia"). Bizarre and stereotypical movements and rituals, for example during meals and at bedtime, are another characteristic of Kanner's autistic children. This is almost never found in children who are simply mentally delayed.

## Differential diagnosis

It must be acknowledged that some young children with neurological disorders, whether mild or severe, also exhibit autistic traits, which should not be confused with Kanner's autism. Kanner's autism has nothing to do with schizophrenia! Childhood schizophrenia, recognized as rare, generally progresses rapidly, so that the increasingly severe deterioration of personality cannot be ignored. Sometimes it's not easy to distinguish autism from deafness. Autistic children are largely unresponsive to many stimuli from the outside world, especially speech, and do not react. Thus, mothers often think that the child cannot hear. Deaf children, on the other hand, lacking the most important tool of interpersonal contact, present some behavioral difficulties, but never autistic behavior. While the autistic child of early childhood (Kanner) simply does not look at the speaking adult or sibling, the gaze of the intelligent, non-brain-affected deaf child is intensely focused on the face and mouth of the speaking adult. The expressive gaze, often accompanied by overly lively facial expressions and gestures, is completely different from the detached gaze of the autistic child. Auditory testing controlled by EEG can also settle the question.

## The Nature of Kanner's Early Childhood Autism

It is debatable whether this clinical picture should be classified among childhood psychoses. It is certain that in the families of individuals with early childhood autism, it is not uncommon to find people who also exhibit clear autistic traits. Moreover, early childhood autism is four to five times more common in males than in females. Initially, Kanner believed that the disorder came from outside and was caused by the family situation, but later he distanced himself from the idea that the emotionally cold mother was the cause. Today, he speaks of an "innate phenomenon," an innate condition. "It's a mystery" is the last word of his wisdom. Kanner reported concordant autistic identical twins of early childhood, another important indication of the constitutional condition. Lempp, on the other hand, believes that early childhood autism is always caused by organic brain damage, meaning it is an "organic psychosyndrome of early childhood." This could be supported by the fact that quite a few autistic children of early childhood develop seizures later on.

## About therapy

It's not surprising that an innate deficiency, namely the inability to establish contact and muteness, the lack of affectivity, can be difficult, if not impossible, to eliminate. Learning capacity is always impaired in the absence of affectivity. If progress is made, it's due to constant devotion and engagement in seemingly nonsensical play of the autistic child. This is where non-directive play therapy celebrates its small victories. One shouldn't impose themselves on these children, but they can accompany their play with words and thereby stimulate them to express something on their own. An experience that Asperger had in Japan seems interesting. There, the issues of autistic children are taken very seriously. The following "psychotherapy" is tried: during the initial treatment hours, clinical psychologists carry the child on their back, without doing anything else with them or asking them anything. This skin-to-skin contact gradually leads the child to enter into human interaction, upon which greater empathy and learning capacity can be built. This entire method probably originated in this country, as here the mother typically carries her child on her back or hip. In this country, certain institutions have specialized in treating early childhood autistic children. Parent associations for autistic children exist in Hamburg (and other cities). Address: Bundesverband Hilfe für das autistische Kind, Bebelallee 141, 2000 Hamburg 60. Phone: 040/511 68 25. The best place for these children would be their own family. For a mother, having an autistic child can be a real torment. She was joyful at the birth of this child, she cares for him and caresses him, gradually she doubts if she's doing everything right, as she receives no affective response. Eventually, her own feelings for the child wither away bit by bit. Who can be surprised by that?


## Prognosis

According to Kanner, the condition of early childhood autism often improves decisively between the ages of 6 and 8. Nevertheless, these children remain remarkable and rarely become school-ready. If few changes are demanded of them and their special habits are taken into account, early childhood autistic children adapt later on many levels. However, even in adulthood, Kanner-type autistics almost always remain remarkable.

# XV/ ASPERGER AUTISM (1982)

Asperger children were particularly notable during their school years for their contradictions: they were intelligent but often failed in school, had a different psyche, were highly thoughtful and observant yet very difficult to discipline, appeared devoid of emotions while being capable of subtle ones. More importantly, they were highly idiosyncratic in their relationships with people, visibly limited and egocentric. This is what led to the name "autistic" - but not in the sense of Bleuler, who called mentally ill schizophrenics autistic, giving this name to the impenetrable wall that separated them from others. Instead, the term "psychopathy" seems appropriate: the condition is clearly innate, visibly independent of environmental factors - the same applies to Kanner autism. In the case of Asperger's autism, heredity is clearly evident: almost without exception, similar traits are found in their ancestry.

## Symptomatology

### Expressive symptoms

These children are quickly recognizable as soon as they enter a room due to their very distinct expressions, which are completely different from the ways in which normal people establish contact with each other. In fact, the term "contact" does not appear in the old child psychology books; it's evident that these characteristics weren't noticed earlier. Autistic children "look" differently from other children. Their gaze doesn't delve into that of the interlocutor; instead, it gets lost in the distance and seems to pass through the other person. It doesn't respond to the interlocutor's efforts to establish a connection. The same holds true for other contact-creating expressions: facial expressions are sparse and sometimes odd. Motor skills are stiff or awkward, lacking fluidity, not quite suited for practical tasks, and sometimes accompanied by stereotypies.

However, when these children are motivated, they can, for a certain period, achieve astonishing feats of skill.


<u>Psychological Abilities</u>

The psychological abilities of autistic children are very typical of early childhood. With unwavering certainty, they judge teachers and other people, and above all, they recognize weaknesses and provoke them: "I am so mean because you are so boring," says a schoolchild to their teacher. It's an apparent contradiction that these children, so socially maladjusted in their behavior, possess such capabilities, whereas other, less gifted children correctly assess adult authority without being able to rationalize it. Observation and intellectual understanding require a distance from human realities, whereas for normal disciplinary behavior, good emotional resonance is more or less sufficient! The psychological talent of these children, described above, is also accompanied by a differentiated examination of consciousness: physical processes, heartbeats, breathing, as well as thought processes, are heard and described accurately in a way that only these intelligent autistic children are capable of.

<u>Behavioral disorders</u>

What has been described so far - linguistic abilities, early abstraction skills, originality of thought, strong spontaneity - essentially involves positive aspects. Now, we need to discuss the unusual and severe behavior problems that autistic children exhibit in their environment. The typical child effortlessly integrates into the surrounding world after small conflicts, quickly resolved, resonating with the situation using healthy instincts, becoming a part of it, understanding it without rationalization. Autistic children, on the other hand, are "completely different," constantly detaching from the situation, from the group. From the very start, they are perceived as strangers and rejected. In the liveliest crowd, they stand apart, engrossed in a book, for example, seemingly unaware of the cheerful commotion around them. But other children, naturally, don't let them be.

The autistic child draws the accumulated aggression of the group. After the class ends, for instance, they vanish into the wild group of their "enemies," helpless against skilled troublemakers, unable to resist in a fair fight. Their only recourse is often to seek revenge, often with clever malice.

The relationship with authority figures, parents, and teachers, is also disrupted. The sense of attitude toward others, which normally develops in a child seemingly on its own, well before conceptual thinking, which is so finely differentiated, precisely adapted, distinguishing familiar from strange, affectionate from rejecting, strict from conciliatory, and "responding" to it, is visibly lacking in the autistic child. Consequently, constant conflicts arise. At times, the boy is grotesquely disrespectful: what others scarcely dare to think, they say directly to the adult's face without hesitation, and they even take pleasure when the other person gets upset.

In education, the educator's emotional affect plays an important role. The child doesn't learn to obey because the educator speaks coldly and intelligently; quite the opposite, the child craves the love and tenderness of the educator - and they're "good" at it - and they try to avoid the educator's negative emotions. Even an infant "understands" the angry and irritated face of their mother and her harsh, even furious, voice, and acts accordingly. And for a long phase of development, it seems to us that the emotional expression of orders and prohibitions is more crucial than intellectual reasoning, but this doesn't apply to the autistic child! It's difficult to discern whether, confined within themselves and lacking humanity, they don't understand others' expressions or if it's precisely this that propels them toward the opposite reaction. In any case, there's often the impression that the child consciously provokes the educator's anger and finds amusement in it (the educator must draw conclusions from this, as we'll explain further).

Further difficulties arise from the fact that the autistic child cannot or will not skillfully imitate and acquire the gestures of daily life that they copy from adults. In the absence of a true motor disorder, it's extremely challenging to teach them how to dress properly, how to tie a knot, how to behave at the table (for instance, they have trouble with greasy disks in soup and forget everything else).

If we attempt to reduce the characteristics of autistic children to a common denominator, we might say that the issue lies in the "deep self," in the "thymic" emotional part of the personality, which explains the disturbance in human relations and in everything that constructs human contact. While some English and German authors think that autism is a cognitive defect, a disorder of apperception (the child is incapable of understanding others' contact and thus reacts poorly), we believe that this explanation is too superficial, i.e., solely in perception; however, intelligent autistics can perceive and describe exceptionally well. In our view, the concern is deeper: in the structure of the personality!

Autistic children generally react paradoxically to their teacher's emotions: they aren't brought to reason by their powerful anger, but they take joy in it and provoke it. This is what Peter Rosegger did as a child, knowing perfectly well how to defy his father's anger, waiting with a mixture of satisfaction and fear for the storm to break. Therefore, it's necessary to meet autistics "with suspended affect," to not inwardly become angry with them, but to calmly face them, even with a cunning spirit. We've found that demanding obedience and compliance from them doesn't achieve much. It's better to establish a general rule that must be followed, for instance in the sense of "A smart boy does it like this...".

The language of our autistics (who, by the way, are exclusively recruited from boys) is very characteristic. While typically the relationship between the speaker and the listener is clearly conveyed by the tone of the voice, volume, tempo, and other qualities that are hard to describe, the language of "my" autistics differs from what one might expect: sometimes monotonously babbling, singing, and shrill, other times overly modulated, like that of a bad actor. But what's even more striking is that at least the basic cases of our type have an especially close relationship with the logic and abstraction of language. They learn to speak earlier than they learn to walk, and they quickly have grammatically well-structured language with subordinate clauses that precisely formulate logical superordination and subordination. Moreover, they often create neologisms, invented in the moment, not taken up by others, so precise and confident, certainly beyond the ordinary, but they can only delight us.

## Curative educational therapy

We are now addressing the important issue of educational therapy for the children we have described. Anyone who has followed the previous explanations will understand that this won't be easy. Autistic children are difficult at home and at school, and they remain so. Even if tests prove that they are much more intelligent than average, they still aren't good students! What they can do, they owe to their own reflection, their own exploration. But they can't learn, they can't submit to the methods presented and demanded by the school. We know children whose understanding of the laws of numbers and their functions borders on genius, yet they perform poorly in calculations at school because they complicate things for themselves, get lost in their own methods, and most of all, vex the teacher by refusing to do things as demanded. And in areas that don't interest them, they are completely unproductive, displaying utter contempt. Added to all this is their lack of respect for authority, even if the teacher doesn't exhibit the typical professional attitude and believes they must punish disrespect towards their highly deserving person. Such behavior from a child must be quite unsettling for the overall group dynamics.

What the educator should do in general is to respect the child as they are - this seems necessary and effective, especially with an autistic boy. There's no need to force them into what they dislike, but rather acknowledge what they do in their own unique way and highlight it before the class to mitigate the tense situation of the mocked and attacked outsider. To some extent, one must "play along": suggest books that advance them in their particular field, discuss it with them; in doing so, it's essential to recognize that the conversation occurs on the same level, not that the teacher or physician can claim authority, but rather that they must confront the critical engagement with the autistic individual.

At this highly intellectual level, it's possible to establish good communication with these intelligent autistic children, yes, lasting lifelong bonds can be formed that also provide a strong emotional background. A word about the emotional domain of these children is necessary here. It's often felt that these children are "insensitive," devoid of feelings, as expressed by the psychiatrist Schröder's school in Leipzig: they can do such things at school and especially at home that one might consider them incapable of empathy. They make life difficult for the mother because they torment her and say brutal things, to the extent that the small family circle can be seriously disrupted. Yet, once again, we observe that such a boy takes care of an animal in a touching manner, putting in a lot of effort for the animal, and often displays deep emotional involvement, albeit most often in secret. Of course, these emotions are often "different," isolated, unique. But above all, they are continually connected to people who understand and respect them in their specificity.

## Social value

Finally, the question of the future of these unique children must be addressed. It's clear that the autistic children in our population are exclusively boys (although Asperger in the USA also identified typical autistic girls). We find this quite explainable: this type can be considered an extreme variant, if you will, a caricature of manhood - with its exaggerated abstraction, extensive loss of reference to reality, detachment from instinct, and excessive specialization - all of which is far removed from "typical feminine capabilities" - much discussion has revolved around gender equality in the United States in the context of women's emancipation.

During puberty, most of these children experience extreme behavioral disturbances. They change schools multiple times because one can no longer tolerate them. If the formal intellectual talent is present thereafter, efforts must be made to get them into higher education and support them through several painful years during their educational struggles, for instance, with the understanding school doctor as an advocate. For the compelling positive sides of the child that the teacher sometimes doesn't even notice, must not be lost! Autistic children urgently need to be trained in their unique abilities during their secondary education, without which they wouldn't have good career prospects. In the later years of high school, the situation generally improves: the talent for abstract and critical thinking comes into play, and the peculiarities of behavior and learning techniques are then tolerated.

While highly gifted children often have great difficulty finding their profession after finishing their schooling, hesitating, doubting, and even changing career paths, young autistics generally orient themselves with an almost dreamlike certainty towards the profession that seems predetermined for them based on their interests, sometimes even from a very young age. Indeed, they draw most of their energy from their self, their "autos."

They often choose highly specialized professions, sometimes even remote ones - in the sciences, and occasionally the arts - and their achievements sometimes border on genius. One mustn't forget that the development of modern science, with its increasingly differentiated specialization, fits these types. Yes, it seems to us that a dash of "autism" is almost necessary for some high-level scientific or artistic achievements: a diversion from what is concretely necessary, simple, and practical, the ability to take new paths of thought and creation, unlearned, unused, and even focusing on a particular domain worked with great dynamism and originality.

Of course, these individuals remain difficult and sometimes eccentric throughout their lives - isn't this the case of the "absent-minded professor," the immortal figure of humor, an autistic, absent-minded, and ridiculously clumsy person only in everyday matters, but often admired in their grandiose works?

The sexual and familial relationships of these individuals also remain difficult and fraught with tension: finding the "you" in love, absorbing oneself in the other - is very challenging for them and often fails. These problems have often been described in modern poetry (by autistic authors who depicted their own difficulties?). But in reality, there are also many tragic events involving such personalities, probably more than with other individuals - confirming the truth that difficult people suffer both from themselves and from others, as Kurt Schneider defined in psychopathy. Even in the pursuit of a profession, things don't always go smoothly. Interests and abilities are often too distant from actual possibilities. Thus, there exist lives that barely and scantily earn the necessities for their bodies and, at the same time, lead a whimsical and fanciful existence, there are also drifters whom nobody cares about and who "haven't committed to anything." But there are also faithful servants who do things above average, with unwavering commitment and extraordinary skills.

But this raises the important question of the social value of difficult individuals who stand out. The example of autistic personalities, in particular, shows that it would be completely erroneous to use the term "inferior" in such a context: that would be a mistake - and it would also hinder the path to therapeutic education! In these cases, however, it can clearly be demonstrated that a child's difficulties and particular capabilities are inseparable, more than that: they are mutually dependent, two sides of the same individuality. It's only through the existence of such characteristics that the diversity of the human world takes shape; and some autistic individuals contribute much more to the world, they are "the salt of the earth"!

Regarding the issues of infantile autism, especially the type described by Kanner, there is a vast literature from many countries. This might be surprising given the rarity of such cases. However, we believe this fact can be explained by the idea that autism is a general human problem. This point will be developed further at the end.

## Humanity in general

We have shown that autistic behavioral disorders can have different origins, which can and must be distinguished, but which nonetheless share similarities both overall and in subtle details. Thus, as we have already mentioned, we can probably assume the existence of an "autism factor" predetermined by constitution.

However, we believe that human beings generally have the capacity to behave in an "autistic" manner. Human existence is marked by a tension of opposites; the human being is deeply rooted in the desire to be alike. Long before the awakening of intellectual faculties, from early childhood, the human child possesses differentiated contact capabilities, being capable of expression and perceiving the expressions of others; the child actively reaches out with a strong dynamism towards others, wanting to be with them. Aristotle defines human existence as follows: man is a "political animal," a creature that forms a community, intertwined with the community in all things, and richly equipped with means of contact.

However, the human being is not only a part of the world, resonating with people and things, to some extent in accordance with the respective environmental situation. The human being is also a "self," anchored within itself, distinct from the world, and at times even in opposition to it. There are phases in development where this becomes particularly pronounced: in certain phases of childhood fear, in the "oppositional phase" of the young child, but especially in the period of self-discovery during puberty (both intellectually and emotionally), during which serious conflicts with the environment can arise precisely because the self is now emerging strongly. Certain experiences can also turn individuals against themselves, making them somewhat "autistic": disappointments, severe sufferings. Expressions such as the experience of depression exhibit similarities with autistic behavior: the vacant gaze, the sense of being cut off from external stimuli. Lastly, a person in a state of creative and spontaneous mental activity also displays "autistic" behavior. Such an individual must to a large extent shield themselves from the external world, from people and things, and turn inward; numerous examples could be provided from poetic descriptions as well as fine arts.

Therefore, it must be acknowledged that humans generally have the potential to behave in an autistic manner, just as they are naturally endowed with tools that allow them to be part of the human community, to absorb the momentary situation, and to "respond" to it in an appropriate manner.

In unfavorable environmental situations and under certain educational conditions, pathological degrees of autism can develop, bordering on psychosis. The fact that the self-observing human being, facing an object, recognizes so many things that are characteristic of themselves is likely the captivating aspect that occupies so many researchers today in an intensive manner.

# AFTERWARD

As a reminder, Lorna Wing (1981) coined the term "Asperger's syndrome" after conducting clinical work with 34 individuals aged 5 to 35, explicitly stating modifications to Hans Asperger's works and descriptions. In my view, Lorna Wing distanced herself significantly from Asperger's original work and instead aimed to emphasize the triad identified previously (Wing & Gould, 1979). She further explained that only 20% of the children she described as having Asperger's syndrome would have an IQ above 70. I have previously discussed this in the book where I commented on Lorna Wing's work (Rebecchi, 2023d), suggesting that there was a kind of conceptual shift, where the true descriptions by Asperger were removed from autism (or were never truly associated), and his name was altered. Moreover, I believe that Hans Asperger's descriptions are not part of the clinical designation "Autism Spectrum Disorder," nor were they even included in the clinical term "Asperger's syndrome." On the contrary, his work has fallen into obscurity. Based on these observations and analyses, I have selected certain elements that I will now discuss.

## Heredity and autism in women

Despite reading numerous publications (books, scientific articles, popular articles) on "autism in females" for several years (of extremely variable quality), I am still not convinced of the relevance of this label or even the existence of the concept as it is presented (that autism would be invisible in girls and women, and that it could be identified by analyzing to what degree the person hides their autism).

In his writings, Asperger (Chapter VII) noted very clearly that autistic mothers possessed the same characteristics as their autistic sons (which led some to believe in the infamous "refrigerator mother" theory), and for him, heredity left no doubt (Chapter XV). This observation was also reported by Kanner in the description of infantile autism. Hans Asperger also emphasized that he had observed girls corresponding to his descriptions in the United States (Chapter XV). Personally and professionally (in research or teaching settings), I have observed the Asperger's autistic profile in girls and women on multiple occasions. This prompts me to question this new profile: should we return to distinct autistic entities as historically existed (Asperger clearly distinguished his autism from Kanner's autism)? Does this mean that some women fit the description of "autism in females" and others do not (so can we still genuinely talk about autism in females)? Could there be multiple "autisms in females"? Furthermore, many autistic men claim to fit this new description of autism, which is based on "masking" or "social camouflage." Does this mean they are not men, then? In my view, masking corresponds to adaptation strategies to a social environment that is often hostile, excluding, and discriminatory for autistic individuals. However, this doesn't mean that autism is "invisible." Asperger repeatedly writes that doctors and teachers do not know how to observe and that they use standardized and inappropriate analytical frameworks, which can create an impression of invisibility. Certainly, women generally have better socioemotional abilities than men, and this holds true in autism as well. It is also observed that social skills follow the curve of intelligence quotient (IQ), with higher IQ correlating to higher social skills. However, I believe this doesn't reflect a difference in the autistic profile but rather a simple neurobiological tendency difference (with exceptions, of course) between men and women.

Moreover, it seems to me that the dichotomy between "autism in females" and "autism in males" often relies on impervious sexual stereotypes from another era (men being portrayed as cold and logical, and women as gentle and decorative). Do some autistic women not regularly hear that they seem cold and aloof? I would be more measured than Fombonne (2020), who caricatures masking by stating "what we see is not actually what we see, but rather what we cannot see," asserting that autism is neither invisible (Dachez & Caroline, 2016) nor difficult to detect. If you have encountered autistic individuals, knowingly or not, men or women, and someone tried to explain to you with A+B that you are incapable of perceiving the difference in these individuals, how would you respond? As I mentioned in the preface, Asperger wrote that once you have learned to identify it, you see it frequently (Rebecchi, 2023a), and it is not about learning to use standardized tests such as the ADOS or ADI-R or the M-CHAT, but about observing the details, what stands out from the ordinary, without applying truncated and inappropriate analyses as is often the case clinically.

Finally, I would add that the descriptions made by Sukhareva (Rebecchi, 2022) are more precise and in-depth regarding the differences between autism in boys and autism in girls (they might even represent the materialization of the idea of extreme male and female brains). I believe that we should stop trying to reinvent the wheel while overlooking extraordinarily relevant and insightful past works.

<u>**Identification, diagnosis and follow-up**</u>

That being said, "visible" does not mean "clinically remarkable," nor visible to everyone. Asperger wrote in 1944 that these children were easily recognizable in educational or pedagogical situations involving free play, real-life situations, and work, and not in an artificial clinical consultation that does not allow for observing the child's free and spontaneous reasoning and productions. According to Asperger (Chapter II), the medical (or clinical) conversation with the child must absolutely not be standardized (meaning that tests, materials, or interview grids using the same objects and asking the same questions with the same words should not be used for all children before comparing their responses). It should, on the contrary, be a "simple" conversation and exchange (which can be one-sided) with the child (but this can also apply to adults) that doesn't necessarily rely solely on spoken language and allows for some freedom. Asperger (Chapter XI) thus discourages behavioral therapies that are merely manipulative strategies to obtain what one desires and emphasizes that respect involves taking time (a lot of time), listening, asking questions to clarify without interpreting what the child says, and taking them seriously (Chapter XII). Asperger also notes that although Kanner-type autistics are almost always remarkable (especially physically) (Chapter XIII), the autistic children he describes primarily perceive themselves (Chapter XIV) through how they interact with others, their different psyche, their evident intelligence despite a lack of academic success, and their behavior that is challenging to manage in the classroom.

In the end, I mostly agree with Asperger's exposition, except for the fact that all these questions would fall within the medical and pathological realm, in addition to the educational and pedagogical sphere. Firstly, I believe that early screening campaigns are futile and that what is visible and "pathological" or "problematic" is already easily detected (and these children are already consulting professionals early in their lives). The issue with the children described by Asperger is therefore not a medical problem, but a societal problem where categorization and binary classification between "normal" and "pathological" occur (and it's specifically on this point that I diverge from Hans Asperger's thinking). Children are educated in very uniform ways, which does not allow slightly different personalities to develop properly and thrive. Therefore, it is entirely possible (and not necessarily difficult) to identify these children outside the medical framework (it can be parents, in daycare, kindergarten, school...) and provide them with support that respects their peculiarities, so that these peculiarities do not become "problematic" (problems related to entirely unsuitable education, somewhat akin to feeding your cat chocolate for every meal). However, we are still far from having created accessible and respectful environments, and I can understand and acknowledge that what is "observable" or "remarkable" for some is still "undetectable" or even "invisible" for others. Furthermore, it is also important to understand, as noted by Plomin, that the influence of genetic factors increases over the course of life, which means that differences and peculiarities amplify with time, like a snowball rolling down a snowy mountain. According to him, by instinct, we "select, modify, or create environments according to our genetic propensities" and "we become our genes as we grow up" (Plomin, 2023). This could also explain why some autistic people experience a decline in social skills over time (Fountain et al., 2023). This thus raises questions about "invisibility" but also the "relevance" of attempting early detection or placing such great importance on an individual's childhood history in diagnostic pathways.

## Education and pedagogy

I believe that the education that Hans Asperger speaks of, which should be offered to the public, is in complete contradiction with what is currently provided in public systems, whether in France or in the United States, for example. I also think that a significant number of difficulties and "behavioral disorders" are provoked by rigid and inadequate school systems. As Asperger indicates (Chapter I), it is futile to follow educational ideologies and pit them against each other without trying for a single moment to understand and know the children. The examples given by Asperger, which remain valid to this day, are telling: why base an entire education on writing when dealing with a dyslexic child? Why force a child with ADHD to sit still for several hours? Why let an autistic child navigate the current educational and pedagogical organization? If Asperger thought that these children were difficult to educate, I, on the contrary, believe that they are easily educable, provided that time and resources are dedicated, and appropriate approaches and environments are offered.

The children described by Hans Asperger understand just and justified rules very well, are curious, and should neither be left to their own devices nor overprotected (as this can also have detrimental consequences, as Professor Asperger reminded us in Chapter VIII). It is also necessary to encourage them to develop their talents, predispositions, and follow their interests (it's generally quite easy to propose cross-disciplinary activities to children by addressing a single theme), without being too directive and by providing them with a benevolent and empowering framework that leads them towards autonomy. This involves an education that allows children to conduct their own research and pursue their own reflections (as proposed by Asperger, Chapter XIV) without seeking to assess development and acquisitions in a standardized manner.

What can greatly facilitate the smooth progress of development and learning for the children described by Asperger is, of course, that the responsible adults create an environment animated by the values of respect for individualities and solidarity, acknowledging the strengths, value, and difficulties of all its members. All these elements will undoubtedly benefit not only Asperger's autistic children but also all children who don't always feel comfortable within the mold. I have chosen not to delve into the topic of gifted individuals (Chapter X), as while there may be specific pedagogical considerations in their education, it does not seem to me that this is as significant a social issue as the ones Hans Asperger echoes. There are obviously connections between the two groups (Asperger speaks of abstract thinking, language, and the strong spontaneity of thought and action), but I would add certain differences (according to Asperger, the question of socialization is the distinguishing criterion), notably the strong self-awareness and awareness of others, as well as the significant creative abilities present in the autistic children he describes. For reference, it is generally accepted that intelligence quotient plays a role in creative abilities up to an IQ range between 85 and 120 (Jauk et al., 2013).

I will conclude this section with a quote from a 1980 preface by Hans Asperger that I have not included in this work:

*"There's no denying that education has become more difficult today than ever before. With today's profound socio-economic changes, many foundations of human behavior have become uncertain and no longer sufficient. Conflicts are everywhere - within human beings who can no longer find their bearings in a changing world, between generations who no longer understand each other, parents giving up leadership and young people no longer willing to be guided by the old ways. The fact that there are conflicts in themselves is not a bad thing. We simply have to learn to understand them in their regularity and find empathetic help".*

## Distinction between autism and "the rest"

As I explained in the afterword of the book on autistic children by Lorna Wing (Rebecchi, 2023d), the differential diagnosis between intellectual disability and autism is complicated, particularly because developmental delays in individuals with intellectual disabilities and/or global developmental delays can lead to difficulties present in the current autistic dyad, which in my opinion does not represent autism at all. As a reminder, the autistic triad described by Wing and Gould (1979) was extracted from around a hundred children, of whom 97% had IQs of less than 70 and 83% had IQs of less than 49. Therefore, even the latest scientific studies on the subject (Thurm et al., 2019; Blacher et al., 2022) firstly explain that parents prefer to receive diagnoses of autism spectrum disorder (ASD) rather than intellectual disability because individuals with autism generally benefit from more comprehensive services. Secondly, it would not be possible to dissociate communication and developmental issues between autism and intellectual disability. In my view, if the differential diagnosis between autism spectrum disorder and intellectual disability (also referred to as intellectual developmental disorder) is so complex, it's because the current conception of autism is unfounded. Unfortunately, this is a point that Professor Hans Asperger emphasized significantly.

He noted (Chapter III) that certain children could exhibit autistic behaviors but without the aspect of uniqueness and distinctiveness reported in his descriptions. Children with cerebral/neurological disorders (Chapter XIII) can also behave in the same way; they might resemble encyclopedias, recalling everything, yet they will be incapable of adapting to life situations (unlike autistics). Even Kanner (Chapter XI) wanted to exclude these children (who almost systematically present severe intellectual disabilities, unlike the children he described) from the autism label, and also distinguish infantile autism from intellectual disability (which, as I mentioned earlier, is not always done; sometimes the two are still treated as a single entity, whether in clinical practice or research). Among the autistic children described by Kanner, few had intellectual disabilities; they did not have physical deformities, not always able to speak, but possessed excellent memory, musical abilities, and specific interests.

As Frankl (Rebecchi, 2023b) does, Asperger insists (Chapter XI) on the distinction between autism and deaf-mute children (as differentiation is not always made, some of these children can exhibit autistic behaviors due to not having access to all their senses, which reduces their interaction with the environment). He also recalls that according to Kanner (see Rebecchi, 2023c), infantile autism is very rare (one child in 5000). These distinctions, contrary to what is often erroneously heard everywhere (perhaps due to a desire for conformity or political correctness), are not meant to level children based on their "utility" or "value." Asperger had absolutely no intention of excluding these children.

## Social value of children with intellectual disabilities

As this section is at the heart of the Hans Asperger controversy, I feel it's important to report what he had to say. In Chapter VI (written in 1938, during the Nazi period and just before the Second World War), he stressed the importance of not regarding the abnormal as inferior, and of not judging children with inferior intellectual development on their intelligence:

*"However, today, allow me not to address the issue from the perspective of the entire nation - which would lead us to mainly discuss the law for the prevention of procreation of subjects affected by hereditary diseases - but from the perspective of abnormal children. The question is what we can do for these individuals. And when we help them with all our dedication, we also render the best service to our nation; not only by preventing these individuals from burdening the national community with their antisocial and criminal acts, but also by seeking to assist them in finding their place as contributors within the living organism of the nation. At the outset, it seems necessary to define a concept: everything that departs from the ordinary, hence "abnormal," does not necessarily have to be "inferior" as a result. (...) In the foregoing, I have described a type whose fundamental abnormality arises from a disturbance in the harmony between intellect and instinct, in the sense of an instinctual disorder. In child psychopathology, there is also a type that embodies almost all the aspects opposite to what has just been described: these children have*

*below-average intellectual development (down to debility), where intelligence is understood as abstract intelligence, while practicality, in short, everything related to instinct, and thus practical utility, as well as emotional values, are relatively better developed. These latter cases are important, or will become so in our context when the 'law for the prevention of offspring affected by hereditary diseases' also comes into effect. When a doctor is called upon to act as an expert in such cases, they cannot make decisions solely based on the outcome of a questionnaire or the score of the intelligence quotient, but primarily based on their understanding of the child's personality, an understanding that takes into account all of the child's capacities, not just abstract intelligence."*

On the other hand, Hans Asperger (this time a text written just before his death, and it doesn't prove his bona fides, but it's a building block to the previous text) also criticized the Nazis and their racial and eugenic ideology (chapter X) :

*"We must strongly refute those who too easily employ the term 'inferior.' The recent periods should have taught us the profoundly inhumane, even deadly consequences that this inevitably brings: the term 'unworthy of life' is not far off in such cases! Yet, those who adopted such an attitude were completely blind to the fact that they themselves, who considered themselves racially and characteristically of high value, were severely abnormal individuals, marked by their cold and unreal ideology as well as by certain other 'psychopathic' traits, thereby excluding themselves from the circle of humanity. One of the most powerful men of the time spoke of 'beasts of intelligence' - was he perhaps mocking himself?"*

From here, I refer readers to the preface and the section titled

'The Controversy' and the subsequent ones to form their own opinion. Personally, it appears quite convoluted to assert that Hans Asperger was a Nazi who aimed to exterminate disabled and/or intellectually impaired individuals. This seems to me to be indicative of an era in which we live in highly comfortable societies without such magnitude of issues to confront, and without the real ability to truly envision what life was like in the first part of the 20th century. All these questions now lead me to discuss the concept of 'normalcy'.

## The norm and the value of difference

According to Asperger, it's important for adults in contact with the autistic children he described to pay attention to their specificities, to what stands out and departs from the ordinary, rather than attempting to study, analyze, observe, or understand them based on a norm, as health professionals often do (Chapter I). And ultimately, it's only by understanding differences that one can truly comprehend the 'normal' (Chapter III). He reminds us (Chapter X), as many other authors and scientists before him have, that all humans, even those who appear most brilliant, are complex beings with contradictions and tensions. He also discusses the well-known and debated idea that 'genius' is linked to 'madness' (both terms are, of course, to be taken in broad senses). According to him (Chapter XII), what deviates from the norm is pathological or diseased, and as I mentioned earlier, I disagree with this notion. In my opinion, what is called 'normal' is a uniform, very limited, and uninteresting construct, and integrating differences that are considered non-pathological could greatly enrich it. This includes recognizing and highlighting the strengths, abilities, and skills of the children he describes.

## Strengths and abilities of Asperger's "autistic psychopaths"

Asperger emphasizes that these children can have and develop strengths, compensate and overcompensate (Chapter I and VI), with the consequences that are well-known. Some might even be capable of exceptional intellectual achievements, and this could be explained by something written in his 1943 thesis and reaffirmed in some of his texts, namely that "superiorities" are linked to "inferiorities," that "advantages" and "difficulties" are inherently connected, they all condition and are inseparable (Chapter VI and XII). Thus, it is impossible to treat and "eliminate" the "weaknesses" and difficulties while hoping to retain only the advantages and qualities (Chapter XII), because all of this forms a coherent whole that is necessary to accept and support in a society that is still hostile to it. These personalities cannot do what is expected of them, they are naturally non-conformist, reject unjustified authoritarianism, demonstrate deep introspection and interoception, are capable of not succumbing to social pressure (even if they are strongly rejected for this reason), are very thoughtful and observant, are highly sensitive (differently from typical sensitivity), possess strong abstract (or practical) thinking, often have artistic or scientific skills, a strong creative potential, dynamism, and originality, have highly developed language (especially in terms of vocabulary), very strong interests, as well as highly developed metacognitive abilities. Thus, support should not focus on reducing what is considered a weakness or difficulty, but rather on socio-professional integration and the flourishing of individuals with autism. It is also important to understand that this doesn't necessarily involve seeking pre-made communities where individuals must abandon their personality (and, in my opinion, this is what often creates issues of integration and mutual understanding) and which often reject them. They appreciate solitude, but that doesn't mean they don't desire relationships (there's a difference between "building a relationship" and "integrating into a community"). Furthermore, they are detached from their environment (which, I believe, is one of the key and specific characteristics of autism described by Hans Asperger), but that doesn't imply they don't live in society and are not part of it; they can enjoy talking (but that doesn't necessarily mean they enjoy small talk or want to engage in exchanges).

My analysis and viewpoint, a subject I have been working on for several years, is that what is referred to as "creative thinking" - or even "creative abilities" - could be the default thinking mode of Asperger's autistic personalities and could visibly manifest the entirety of characteristics described by Hans Asperger. This leads us to ponder what autism truly is, or rather, the various conceptions of autism.

### What is autism (really)?

In my opinion, the different current conceptions (not necessarily mutually exclusive) of autism are:

- **A pathology or disorder** characterized by the symptom dyad from the Diagnostic and Statistical Manual of Mental Disorders (DSM), which is found in numerous genetic syndromes or developmental disorders, and which is not associated with any strength, ability, or advantage (this is the prevailing and current conception, and within this framework, debates over the use of terms like "disorder," "pathology," or "illness" - or others - are, in my opinion, unfounded as the conception remains the same). This is notably the perspective of Lorna Wing. This conception supports the idea that autism is the result of developmental issues (resulting in the DSM's dyad of problems) and would not be a distinct "neurotype," meaning a brain that functions differently and exists apart from the dyad. In this conception that refutes the idea of a different cognition, autism can be treated and cured, and the objective remains the search for treatments and/or therapies, although we often hear new terminology from professionals and researchers such as "improvement in quality of life" to overlook this fact. This conception is entirely based on the notion of diagnosis through clinical observation, as the DSM's dyad is only characterized by a set of behaviors.

- **A mindset** (Schröder - Chapter X - defines it as the ability to be with others, the perception of what a person emits and radiates toward oneself, allowing engagement with them, even attachment with love and loyalty) that is specific, not necessarily abnormal, which complements the state of being in communication with people, and the transition between this previous state and the state of autism occurs freely (even if with difficulties or discomfort). This is notably George Frankl's perspective.

- **A (altered) state of consciousness** (Dittrich - 1980 - defines it as a marked deviation in subjective experience that alters an individual's psychological functioning and provokes changes in mood, self-perception, environment, time, and space).

- **A type of personality** (which can be defined as "The dynamic organization within an individual of common traits, patterns of behavior, values, interests, plans, and motives, self-understanding and world view, abilities, and emotional patterns that shape characteristic behavior and thought. All of the individual's systems that develop and interact to create unique and shared characteristics of the person," Matsumoto, 2009), even a new dimension of personality (Wakabayashi et al., 2006), in addition to openness, conscientiousness, extraversion, agreeableness, and neuroticism (McCrae & Costa, 1990).

- **A set of traits and characteristics** present in everyone to varying degrees. This is notably the perspective of Plomin.

Also, some people believe that, in the light of these last two conceptions, autism is an ostracizing and pathologizing social label applied to individuals who resist social conditioning and collective identities (Ludwig, 2022).

Hans Asperger explains that "autistic behaviors" can be found in numerous people across various situations (neurological disorders, anxiety, disappointments, intense suffering, creative states, spontaneous mental activity...) and thus, it is possible for all humans to exhibit autistic behavior (Chapter XI), even from early childhood (Chapter II). He also believes that there exist pathological degrees of autism (and the corollary would therefore be that non-pathological

242

degrees of autism exist as well). This is why, in his view, a degree of autism would be almost indispensable for certain high-level scientific or creative achievements (Chapter XIV), as these involve creativity, originality, innovation, dynamism (abilities he associates with autism). Therefore, I believe that Asperger's autistic perspective corresponds to a mixture of the five different conceptions I previously listed. However, I remain convinced that the first proposition is the least relevant when discussing the children he described, and that the autism spectrum disorder is probably the most distant autistic conception from all of this, and the least appropriate definition with a set of elements that can be found in many things like social anxiety, burnout, or even schizophrenia, without necessarily indicating a different neurotype. As Baron-Cohen (2017) points out, no definition of the term "disorder" is suitable for describing autism, and this term should only be used when there is nothing positive about the person's state, or even if, in case of environmental change, the person remains incapable of functioning. He thus emphasizes the relevance of using the word "difference," as autism leads to a difference in functioning, and autistic individuals simply develop differently (and sometimes even better - not in terms of value but rather performance - which is why using the term "disability" is also irrelevant).

I therefore think that depending on perspectives, angles of analysis, definitions chosen, these different conceptions are defensible, but they don't necessarily describe the same thing. Additionally, I also encourage researchers to foster more intercultural studies (outside the framework of the autism spectrum disorder conception) on the subject in order to compare conceptions and representations across the world.

Also, it would not seem inconsistent to differentiate developmental disorders and executive function disorders (which lead to the characteristics of the dyad, akin to intellectual developmental disorder) from autism and ADHD (which might be worth renaming), both of which present "advantages" unlike the two preceding disorders.

## References

Baron-Cohen, S. (2017). Editorial Perspective: Neurodiversity—a revolutionary concept for autism and psychiatry. Journal of Child Psychology and Psychiatry, 58, 744-747. https://doi.org/10.1111/jcpp.12703

Blacher, J., Baker, B. L., & Moody, C. T. (2022). Autism Spectrum Disorder Versus Intellectual Disability. Differential Diagnosis of Autism Spectrum Disorder, 22-43. https://doi.org/10.1093/med-psych/9780197516881.003.0002

Dachez, J., & Caroline, M. (2016). La différence invisible. Delcourt, Dl.

Dittrich, A. (1998). The standardized psychometric assessment of altered states of consciousness (ASCs) in humans. Pharmacopsychiatry 31, 80–84. https://doi.org/10.1055/s-2007-979351

Fombonne, E. (2020). Camouflage and autism. Journal of Child Psychology and Psychiatry, 61(7), 735–738. https://doi.org/10.1111/jcpp.13296

Fountain, C., Winter, A. S., Cheslack-Postava, K., & Bearman, P. S. (2023). Developmental Trajectories of Autism. Pediatrics. https://doi.org/10.1542/peds.2022-058674

Jauk, E., Benedek, M., Dunst, B., & Neubauer, A. C. (2013). The relationship between intelligence and creativity: New support for the threshold hypothesis by means of empirical breakpoint detection. Intelligence, 41(4), 212–221. https://doi.org/10.1016/j.intell.2013.03.003

Ludwig, F. L. (2022). Why Deindividuation Resisters Are Ostracised - Autism as a Social Construct. http://franklludwig.com/deindividuationresisters.html

Matsumoto, D. (Ed.). (2009). The Cambridge dictionary of psychology. Cambridge University Press.

McCrae, R. R., & Costa, P. T., Jr. (1990). Personality in adulthood. Guilford Press.

Plomin, R. (2023). Les parents et l'école influent peu sur la réussite des enfants. L'Express. https://www.lexpress.fr/sciences-sante/robert-plomin-les-parents-et-lecole-influent-peu-sur-la-reussite-des-enfants-D2AB2XQ4DNAYRGFUDAWZTHY5OU/

Rebecchi, K. (2023a). Autistic children - Hans Asperger. Kindle Direct Publishing.

Rebecchi, K. (2022). Autistic children - Grunya Sukhareva. Kindle Direct Publishing.

Rebecchi, K. (2023b). Autistic children - George Frankl. Kindle Direct Publishing.

Rebecchi, K. (2023c). Autistic children - Leo Kanner. Kindle Direct Publishing.

Rebecchi, K. (2023d). Autistic children - Lorna Wing. Kindle Direct Publishing.

Thurm, A., Farmer, C., Salzman, E., Lord, C., & Bishop, S. (2019). State of the Field: Differentiating Intellectual Disability From Autism Spectrum Disorder. Frontiers in psychiatry, 10, 526. https://doi.org/10.3389/fpsyt.2019.00526

Wakabayashi, A., Baron-Cohen, S., & Wheelwright, S. (2006). Are autistic traits an independent personality dimension? A study of the Autism-Spectrum Quotient (AQ) and the NEO-PI-R. Personality and Individual Differences, 41(5), 873–883. https://doi.org/10.1016/j.paid.2006.04.003

Wing, L., & Gould, J. (1979). Severe impairments of social interaction and associated abnormalities in children: Epidemiology and classification. Journal of Autism and Developmental Disorders, 9(1), 11–29. https://doi.org/10.1007/BF01531288

Wing L. (1981). Asperger's syndrome: a clinical account. Psychological medicine, 11(1), 115–129. https://doi.org/10.1017/s0033291700053332